Front Cover: *Dragonfly* (in the style of Madhubani) by Rinal Parikh

Rinal Parikh's art reflects the heritage and vibrant culture of her native India. A self-taught artist, Rinal draws on a childhood fascination with color and composition, portraying spontaneity and energy with saturated color in various media.

Her subjects are influenced by life in India, and she studies the many different styles of Indian painting that vary from state to state: "Although they are from the same country," she says, "they are very different from each other – I find it intriguing." Rinal's work has appeared in India in group exhibitions and on magazine covers. In the United States, she made her debut with a solo exhibit at The Creative Living Room in Swarthmore. Her work has featured in several solo and group exhibits in the tri-state area and has won several awards. She enjoys teaching children and adult watercolor classes at her home studio in Wallingford, PA.

"I believe in always improving myself, learning from every stage in life and from nature. I love incorporating several mediums into my art. Painting is my way of expressing my feelings."

Originals, Limited edition Giclee, Digital Prints, Art classes, and Studio visits:

www.rinalparikh.com
info@rinalparikh.com
rinal.parikh@gmail.com

Praise for *Lost and Found*

"This book is much, much more than a widow memoir. The first part takes you through the touching and painful story of the author's grief. It is raw and honest - the way a good friend would share. I wished I had kept a journal after my husband died, but Ellen Monsees' experiences, word choices, descriptions, and feelings so accurately captured what I felt, that I feel like she wrote one for me.

After completing the Grief Recovery Method and becoming a practitioner, the author went on to develop her own technique called The PPF Method. In the second part of the book she gently explains how she uses it to assemble the mosaic of her new life by connecting her past, present, and future selves. She shows how you can apply it, too. I immediately tried it out on a job decision I had been debating about for two weeks. In less than 5 minutes I knew the right thing to do and have never looked back. PPF is a powerful tool and it works! I can't wait to do more."

Bonnie Neubauer, widow, and author of *The Write-Brain Workbook Revised & Expanded, 400 Exercises to Liberate Your Writing*

"'*Life can only be understood backward, but it must be lived forward.*' Soren Kierkegaard

As a trauma therapist, I know that experiencing the anguish of loss and its accompanying grief is grueling enough. Layering a traumatic death into the mix requires a journey through the murkiness of one's very being. Traumatic grief attacks one's self-definition in ways that few other life events can, and often requires that you experience distress, isolation and a desperate longing for "what was" as painful first steps. Part 1 of Ellen's memoir provides a candid and insightful roadmap to surviving loss and wading through the initial steps of trauma and grief. In Part 2, Ellen describes her re-awakening and reconciliation processes – including letting go - not of her memories - but rather of her attachment to the past, as well as her courage to imagine and take steps toward a new, joyful life without her beloved husband, John. This book is the very embodiment of Kierkegaard's thesis of the necessity of both backward reflection and forward movement - a very poignant and inspirational read for those experiencing grief and loss, and for those professionals and loved ones wanting to help them."

Stephanie Schneider, MS, LPC

Quotes about Ellen from people who have worked with her:

"She has the most compassionate, generous heart of anyone I've ever known."

"I think she's the warmest, most genuine person I've ever met."

"People are drawn to her because of her friendly, interested, down-to-earth nature."

"I feel completely understood and accepted by her."

"Ellen is an effective communicator, able to express information in practical, understandable terms."

Facebook Reviews:

"It is very difficult to restart and change your career, especially after 50. I completed my resume, went on a few interviews, but I felt insecure and also worried about my age. Procrastination and despair set in. I decided to meet with Ellen to assist me though this road block. First, Ellen discussed my life goals and gave me exercises to help me re-focus my life plan. After working with Ellen, I have regained the energy and motivation to begin my new career path."

"Working with Ellen has played an integral role in identifying my goals and creating short- and long-term plans to reach them. She knows my core values and the themes that I'd like to weave through my life's fabric, and she reminds me of them, keeping me on track and accountable to myself. We explore ideas and put the pieces together, figuring out what is most important to me, and how I can structure my life to minimize the overwhelm and create space for the people and things I truly love. Sitting down with Ellen on a regular basis gives me the chance to check in, recognize my progress, and re-evaluate. Since beginning my work with her, I've gained so much direction and confidence! Thanks, Ellen!"

"Ellen and I started our life coaching relationship about a year and a half ago. It was at a time in my life where things that had been "normal" were all changing - my youngest going to college, my marriage fell apart, and my job of 15 years was coming to an end. Ellen is not a therapist - she's so much more. She listened to where my life was and the changes that were happening. She then came up with exercises and assignments (for lack of a better word) to help me get to my "new normal." We had discussions at a pace that worked for me. She was patient and non-judgmental, listened well, and helped me get on a path that made sense for the period of life I was in and where I wanted to head. While the words may sound cliché, they are no less true. Our coaching relationship has been invaluable. Whenever you find yourself at a crossroads and need help with the path to your "new normal", Ellen is an awesome person to have in your corner."

LOST *and* FOUND

Finding A Joyful Life After Loss

Ellen Landsburg Monsees

Lost and Found

Finding A Joyful Life After Loss

Copyright © 2018, Ellen Landsburg Monsees

The views expressed by the author in reference to specific people in their book represent entirely their own individual opinions and are not in any way reflective of the views of Capucia, LLC. We assume no responsibility for errors, omissions, or contradictory interpretation of the subject matter herein.

Capucia, LLC does not warrant the performance, effectiveness, or applicability of any websites listed in or linked to this publication. The purchaser or reader of this publication assumes responsibility for the use of these materials and information. Capucia, LLC shall in no event be held liable to any party for any direct, indirect, punitive, special, incidental, or any other consequential damages arising directly or indirectly from any use of this material. Techniques and processes given in this book are not to be used in place of medical or other professional advice.

No part of this book may be reproduced or transmitted in any form, or by any means, electronic or mechanical, including photography, recording, or in any information storage or retrieval system without written permission from the author or publisher, except in the case of brief quotations embodied in articles and reviews.

Published by:
Capucia, LLC
211 Pauline Drive #513
York, PA 17402
www.capuciapublishing.com

ISBN: 978-1-945252-45-7
Library of Congress Control Number: 2018958733

Cover Design: Ranilo Cabo with photo by Rinal Parikh
Layout: Ranilo Cabo
Editor and Proofreader: Simon Whaley
Book Midwife: Carrie Jareed

Printed in the United States of America

TABLE OF CONTENTS

Acknowledgments 1
Introduction 3

Part 1: Loss and Recovery 7
    Chapter 1: Everything Changed 9
                    Don't Turn the Key 9
                    The What-if's and If-only's 12
                    Post-mortem Rituals 12
                    Now What? Adjusting to Life without John 15
                    All the Stuff 17
                    Most Surprising: Losing My Identity 24
                    The Invasive Vine of Grief 29
                    Riding the Waves 32

    Chapter 2: Clueless and Searching 35
                    Widowhood is a Detour. Where's My GPS? 35
                    Going Through the Motions and Losing Time 37
                    Working Through Grief 40
                    Monumental, Mundane Adjustments 42

	Figuring Out Self-care	43
	Menopause + Grief = Anxiety	45
Chapter 3:	Our Relationship	47
	Why Did We Become Us?	47
	Our First Date	49
	The First of Many Birthday Extravaganzas	51
	Summers with Ponies	51
	International Travel	53
	Halloween	55
	Thanksgiving	57
	Vermont	58
Chapter 4:	Isolation: Motives and Methods	61
	Alone in a Crowd	61
	At Work	62
	The Shame of Grief	63
	Was I Failing at Grief?	65
	Loss of Traditions	69
	Retreating from Life	70
	Grief, My Constant Companion	73
	The Weight of His Absence	75
Chapter 5:	Beginning to Recover (But Not Quite)	79
	Pretenses	79
	Glimpses of Sunlight	80
	What's Next?	83
Chapter 6:	*This* is Recovery	89
	I Am More Than My Grief	89
	Releasing the Burden	91

	You Can't Hide from Grief 93
	Grief is Emotional 94
	Consequences of Unrecovered Grief 95
	Myths and False Beliefs.. 96
	Have I Recovered? How Do I Know?..................... 99
Chapter 7:	Looking for a New Normal 101
	Moving Through Grief.. 101
	Okay, I've Moved Through Grief. Now What?... 103
	Stuck in Thought Without Action 104

Part 2: Finding My Joyful Life...107

Chapter 8:	Stranded in a New Land 109
	Jettisoning My Career 110
	Addressing the Physical Ramifications of Grief 111
	Creating and Picking Up New Pieces.................... 114
	Choosing to Live Intentionally 117
Chapter 9:	The PPF Method™ 121
	My Past Selves 121
	My Present Self... 128
	My Future Selves 129
Chapter 10:	Bringing the Selves Together................................... 131
	Being My Own Best Friend 132
	Negotiating Among My Selves................................ 134
	Seeking Balance 134
	The Four Elements of a Healthy Relationship.... 136
	The Power of Forgiveness 136

Chapter 11: Loving My Whole Self,
       Loving Myself Whole 139
       Meditation as a Pathway 139
       Broken is Perfection 142
       Healing a False Belief: "I Am Not Creative" 142
       Adjusting Expectations and Practicing
           Self-kindness 146
       Sticking to the Plan 146
       Using The PPF Method to Make
           Short-term Decisions 147
       Dual Future Selves 149
       Daily Meditations and Affirmations 149

Chapter 12: Revisiting and Revising my
       Visions of Future Ellen 151
       Acting As If 152
       Positive Self-talk 153
       Thoughts on Failure 154
       Thoughts on Fear 155
       Taking my Time 156
       Don't Forget Joy! 157

Chapter 13: I am a Work in Progress 161
       Manifesting My Best Future, Choice
           by Choice 165

Epilogue 167
About the Author 169
Connect with me! 171

ACKNOWLEDGMENTS

I could not have written this book without the people who helped me muddle through the darkness of grief until I was able to walk in the light once again. My parents, Vivian and Norman Landsburg, modelled a relationship steeped in love, respect, humor, and mutual support – giving me a foundation that allowed me to be both independent and interdependent as a wife, and to have the kind of marriage that provided true intimacy. My sister, Barbara Farabaugh, was my lighthouse even when I was flailing about in the open seas of despair; knowing that she was keeping a steady eye on me kept me grounded and secure. The love from my brother, Steven Landsburg, my brother-in-law Tom Farabaugh, and my niece Cayley Landsburg helped buoy my spirits when I felt myself sinking. Lisa Lee is the best friend anyone could have: with a gentle hand and complete acceptance, she saw to it that I engaged with the world around me but at my own pace, saving me from my desire to withdraw from life. So many friends helped by allowing me to talk about John and keep his spirit alive through stories; there are too many to name individually here, but I hope you know who you are – the ones I see face-to-face and the ones who are there for me on social media as well.

The actual writing of this book owes its start to Maia Danziger, whose Relax & Write workshops were the birthplace of some of the deepest realizations and admissions of my fears and emotions. But the structure and completion of this work would not have come about without Christine Kloser and her My Time To Write program. To Christine, Carrie Jareed, Tammy Burke, and my transformational author community, I am both humbled and exalted by your love, belief, and acceptance. Thank you.

INTRODUCTION

On the Friday before Thanksgiving in 2008, my husband died. It was sudden and unexpected, and in that moment, the person I had been ceased to exist. This book documents my odyssey through the dark labyrinth of grief, back into the light of recovery – and beyond, to a new me and a new life. Having taken that emotional journey of grieving, I wasn't able to go back to being the same person I had been. Because I had changed, much of my life didn't make sense anymore. So my exploration continued, while I figured out how to find my new path and follow it. As it happens, I devised a practical method of recreating my life that works not only for me but also for others.

One of the things that I found helpful while I was grieving was reading memoirs written by other widows, so I wanted to share my story in the hope that someone else could read it and perhaps feel less alone in their pain. Once I realized I had even more to share, that I could help people not just let go of pain but embrace a vibrant and hopeful existence, my determination to publish became stronger.

Much of what I learned about recovering from grief came from The Grief Recovery Institute® (www.griefrecoverymethod.com). I have gone through their training to become a Certified Grief Recovery Specialist® and feel both privileged and humbled to be able to help others let go of the pain of grief and move beyond loss.

Grief comes in many forms, in addition to sadness. It can be fear, anxiety, illness, sleeplessness, or hopelessness. And loss comes in many forms. In fact, there are over forty life experiences that may result in feelings of loss and grief. Sometimes it's a death. Sometimes it's divorce, or the end of a romantic relationship. Sometimes it's an empty nest. Sometimes it's retirement, or moving, or a change in health or financial circumstances. And, sometimes, it's just a realization that you're not finding joy or fulfillment in your daily life. If you've ever looked around and thought, "How did I get here? This isn't what I wanted out of life," or if you've just had a feeling that your life is out of your control and don't know how to take back the reins, then this book can help.

Whether you need to create a new world because your old one has been shattered by loss, or you want to shatter your old world because it's just not working for you, this book can help. Perhaps you need a new normal, or perhaps you're in a situation that has made you realize you can embrace a new normal. Maybe you see life as broken or empty, due to changes in circumstance or awareness. Maybe you feel lost but don't know where to begin to make things better. Maybe you feel like you're on autopilot and the days are something to be gotten through, but you yearn for days of interest and happiness and purpose. Are you on the cusp of a new act but don't know your lines or cues? Do you feel adrift, yet stuck? This book can help.

INTRODUCTION

I want you to feel normal. I want you to know that you are not alone, that you are loved, that you can feel joy again. I want you to understand that you have access to all of the moments of joy you have ever experienced. I want you to be able to utilize those moments to create a better frame of mind and attitude. I want you to see that you have choices and control in your life, and you have the ability to create a better present and future for yourself.

This book can help you if you are religious or if you are not. The principles of my technique for rebuilding your life don't depend on any particular set of beliefs. However, much of the content of this book is very personal. I will share my truth, in the hope that it resonates with yours. And to begin, I want to let you know that I believe in the interconnectedness of things. I don't believe in divine purpose, a master plan, or destiny. I believe we are part of the universe, and it is a part of us. That we are both the source of and the product of all things. I believe in the conservation of matter and energy. I believe that when we die, we are transformed but don't disappear. Our atoms revert to the cosmic Matter and our souls revert to the cosmic Energy – we disintegrate, lose individuality, and once more become indistinguishable but tangible parts of all that Is.

I believe that my husband is stardust. Dust to dust. He was a unique coalescence of matter and energy, both of which now have dispersed. This does not mean that I no longer have a relationship with him. It does not make him less real. It makes him – all of us – a part of All, interconnected and essential. His individuality remains in every memory and every life that he touched, every path he may have altered.

We all revert to stardust, but that does not negate the value of our lives. I celebrate the wonder of atoms forming molecules forming flesh. I celebrate the miracle of energy transforming to bioelectric impulses. Thought and feeling are real, and no less real just because they are impermanent.

I believe we are all part of one divine. We can tap into the source, we can feel it and measure by it, but there is an element of perceived chaos and randomness – and that is what makes it so important that we choose kindness, order, and compassion, and gives us a moral imperative to do the right things, be ethical and good.

I believe that much of what determines your happiness and satisfaction in life is your attitude. Focus is the key. An optimist doesn't ignore the bad things; she simply recognizes that there are good things as well, and chooses to focus her attention on those good things as much as she can.

The Grief Recovery Method teaches us to become emotionally complete in our relationships with others, to repair regrets and let go of blame, and to express and release significant emotions. The PPF Method has its beginnings in those same principles, but applies them to your relationship with yourself. It will teach you to recognize, value, and create your life's mission. Applying the lessons in this book can help you realize your most centered, fulfilling, productive life and manifest the future self of your deepest desire.

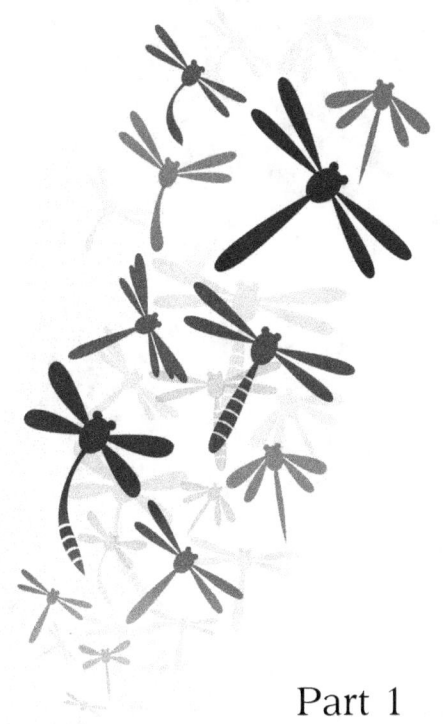

Part 1

Loss and Recovery

CHAPTER 1

Everything Changed

Don't Turn the Key

On November 21, 2008 – the Friday before Thanksgiving – my life was shattered. Everything I knew, everything I dreamed, everything I hoped, everything I expected no longer existed. But I didn't know that yet. What I did know was that my husband was suddenly, unexpectedly, inexplicably dead.

John was 46 years old. He was diabetic and was prone to high blood pressure, but both of those conditions were being managed through lifestyle and medication. He was healthier than I'd ever known him. He worked out at the gym at least four times a week, he ate nutritious low-carb foods, and he hadn't had a drop of alcohol since his diagnosis several years before.

Then I came home one evening to find him lifeless on the kitchen floor.

He'd been away for a few days on a business trip, where he'd been working on a case as an attorney for the US Environmental Protection Agency. We'd talked on the phone each evening, and just the night before had ended our call with "I love you." I was happy that he was coming home; I knew he'd arrive before me, since I was planning an evening out at dinner and a play with a girlfriend. But it was comforting to know that I'd be sleeping with him in our bed again that night.

I pull the car into the driveway, put it in park, turn off the headlights. Long day, but what a nice evening. After work I met Carolyn for dinner at a Cuban restaurant, then we saw a play at the Arden Theatre. It's a little after midnight on Friday, and I'm glad to be home. John came back from his business trip today. I wonder if he's still awake.

As I walk up the path to the kitchen door, I hold my key in my hand. The kitchen light is on, and I can see in through the glass of the door.

Something's different. Is that …? Oh God, John's lying on his back on the floor. He's so ridiculous. He saw me drive up and he's playing a stupid joke – it's so stupid.

I put the key in the lock. No. Don't turn the key. If I turn the key everything will change. My world will end. I stand, frozen. Don't turn the key! I am standing beside myself. My now self is standing beside my then self, shouting: DON'T. TURN. THE. KEY.

She turns the key, she steps over the threshold. "John. John, this is dumb. Get up. Very funny, ha ha. John? John are you okay? John!"

"Okay, if this is a joke, stop it right now. I'm picking up the phone to call 911. If it's a joke, tell me now."

That's when she stopped being herself, when she separated from her life. She heard herself speak into the phone, watched herself try to revive him with CPR. His eyes, open. His skin with spots of gray. His mouth, sour with bile. Please Please Please Please Please Please Please.

Nothing. An ambulance, paramedics. Police officer. Is there someone you can call?

Call? It's midnight, who can I call? Barbara – too far away. Lisa, I'll call Lisa. She's there in 15 minutes, sitting with me on the couch.

You need to call a Funeral Home now.

What? I don't know funeral homes. Everything is happening at a distance, through a wall of gelatin. Ok, pick a funeral home. One I'll be able to find with my bad sense of direction.

Make a list. Who to call. Call Barb. Call Rob. To tell him his brother's dead. Ok. What? What? Oh my God I feel sick.

My world has shifted on its axis, everything is wobbly, surreal. This isn't my world, this isn't my life. I've slipped into the wrong universe, the wrong alternate reality. This isn't my dimension. This isn't. This isn't. How do I get back? I turn in circles, dizzy, lost. I forget to breathe.

I watch as she tries to navigate, unable to reach her, unable to help. She will have to take each halting, crippled step on her own.

I told you not to turn the key.

This is what I pieced together, after the fact: John and his colleague had driven home in their government-issued loaner car from Virginia to Philadelphia, arriving at their office mid-afternoon. He got on the commuter train to our suburban town, then walked the ½ mile from the train station (as he did daily) carrying his duffel bag and wearing a backpack, both of which were heavily packed with clothes and file folders.

He got home, dropped his bags in the living room, and walked into the kitchen to feed the cat. At that point, he had a massive heart attack and dropped dead. I found him six to eight hours later.

The What-if's and If-only's

For a long time, I was plagued with thoughts of what happened, and what could have changed the outcome. What if he hadn't walked from the train? What if he hadn't been carrying such a heavy load of luggage? What if I had been home, would I have been able to help him? If he'd gotten to a hospital, would that have made a difference?

If only I hadn't gone out that night. If only I had picked him up at the train station. If only he'd rested after he got home. If only he'd taken better care of himself from an earlier age, maybe his heart wouldn't have given out. If only he'd learned better how to deal with stress, if only he'd meditated, if only he'd had a better diet or better genes and never developed diabetes.

Post-mortem Rituals

I'd been lucky. I was 49 years old and had never had to think about planning a funeral. People I loved had died, but they were all older than me and none were immediate family. Grandparents, aunts, uncles. It was sad but not devastating, tragic but not unexpected.

All of a sudden, I needed to make decisions I was ill prepared for. John and I had been married for 16 years. We had no children. He had been brought up in a Catholic home but had vigorously rejected all organized religion. I often snickered at his avowed atheism, since he spent an awful lot of energy being angry at a God that he claimed not to believe in. He had been expelled from CCD (Catholic religious education) when he argued with the teacher about evolution. He held a grudge against the church. It frustrated and angered him when things didn't work, when he saw injustice, when he didn't see immediate rewards for following the rules. And he blamed God – the God he didn't believe in. I was agnostic, more prone to Buddhist or Taoist principles than the Judeo-Christian culture predominant in my childhood. Perhaps if we'd had kids we might have been involved in some form of faith community, but being childfree we never felt the need for that in our lives.

Funerals are about ritual, and I didn't have many to fall back on. I felt sure of three things. First, John wouldn't want anything remotely religious. Second, that he had hated funerals and wouldn't want a formal rite of any sort. And third, that he would want to be cremated.

John was an avid fan of horror books and movies. Not slasher films, but demons and vampires and zombies. He'd actually told me, more than once, that if he died before me and I ever saw him I should know it wasn't him, it was a zombie, and I should shoot him or whack him with a shovel, and be sure to aim for the head. He was very uneasy in cemeteries. I find them peaceful oases – I like to walk among the headstones, wondering about the people, seeing the different styles of symbols and writing on the monuments. I think he was always afraid that someone there would take exception to his presence and rise up to object. There was no question that cremation was the way to go, because knowing that his body could never be reanimated into a zombie would be important to him. I shared that thinking with several of his close friends, and the reaction was always the same: a chuckle followed by vigorous nodding of the head.

I know that funerals are for the living, not the dead. But it was important to me to honor the things that he felt very strongly about. And, not being traditionally religious myself, it wasn't a hardship for me to forego the usual ceremony. Except that meant I didn't have a roadmap to follow.

So, I chose a funeral home. I hadn't had any experience or connection with any close by. How to pick? Now, keep in mind, I was sitting on my couch an hour after finding my husband dead on the kitchen floor. My best friend, who had gotten out of bed to drive over and be with me, was sitting beside me and helping me get through each moment. Someone (I don't remember who; it might have been the coroner or police officer) gave her a list of funeral homes and an instruction. We needed to call one, now. Because a funeral home had to send someone out to the house and take the body away. I was completely dazed and could barely focus my vision on the printed list.

I have a terrible sense of direction, and this all happened just a few years before GPS on phones and in cars became the norm. So how did I choose a funeral home? I picked one that wasn't too far away and was very easy to get to. I knew the road it was on and I wouldn't be likely to get lost getting there. That was the only thought I had – I must pick a place I could find easily.

Because I grew up in a Jewish family, albeit a largely nonobservant one, there are certain rituals that give me comfort on momentous occasions. Although John and I were married by a judge, we stood under a chuppah (a marriage canopy), and we broke the glass to cries of "*mazel tov!*", and at the reception we danced a hora to *Hava Nagilah*, because those are the hallmarks of a wedding to me.

When John died, I needed a shiva, the Jewish ritual where people gather to support the family and remember the deceased. So I had what I called a "faux shiva" since it lacked any of the usual religious aspects of prayer or even strong cultural traditions, such as covering mirrors.

The house was filled with family, friends, and coworkers. There were so many wonderful stories told, and lots of laughter as people recalled amusing anecdotes and told each other about practical jokes he had pulled. It was sad but joyful, and wonderful to experience all of the love for this complicated, silly, angry, cynical, loyal, passionate, loving man, but …

… what I realized in that week after his death, was that nobody else in the world knew the John that I knew. They knew parts of him, they saw particular sides of him, they knew him in different roles he had played as coworker, mentor, friend. But they each knew only a slice of who he was. And that made me feel inexpressibly sad and isolated. I saw that I was completely alone in missing MY John, and that there was no one else in the world who missed the same person I did. His brother came closest, but just as I didn't know the John he knew, he didn't know mine either. And that left me desolate.

Now What? Adjusting to Life without John

My life up to now had been relatively devoid of grief and bereavement. I'd certainly never experienced a loss even close to the magnitude of this one. Losing a member of one's household – whether a spouse, a parent, a sibling, or a roommate – is a loss that's compounded by the myriad changes, from tiny to profound, that reoccur every single day. From waking up alone, to cooking for one, to now having to be the one to put out the trash, to not having that partner to turn to for advice and support … every moment served up fresh reminders that he was gone.

I didn't know what to do. I was sad, depressed, angry, confused, lonely, anxious. I did all of the things I could think of to help me process my emotions and "get over" the grief of losing John. I read books about grief and bereavement, especially memoirs written by widows. I went to therapy, seeing first a psychologist then a clinical social worker. I journaled, spewing my thoughts and feelings onto the page. I found some online social networks for grievers and participated in discussions there. I was lucky enough to have a loving family and a lot of good, supportive friends – and even luckier that many of them happened to be single women, so my social life didn't suffer and I wasn't always stuck at home alone.

But all of those things were only helpful in the moment. They allowed me to blow off a little steam, to feel a bit less isolated and crazy, to have the illusion that I was going to get over this. All together, these things didn't help me recover from my grief. But they did help make me strong enough to *carry* the burden of my pain. It would be almost six years before I learned there was a way to actually recover and *release* the burden of that pain. You'll learn about that in Chapter 6.

My grief wasn't only due to missing my husband. I did miss him, terribly. I still do. But that grief was increased by so many secondary losses. I lost John. I also lost our life together, the future I expected, my perspective, my innocence, my sense of security, my dinner companion, my travel buddy, my sharer of private jokes, my biggest cheerleader, and my sounding board.

His absence was shocking. Any time I experienced or remembered something good, it immediately turned to pain because he wasn't there to share it. Even something as simple as seeing his favorite flowers bloom in the yard was a knife to the heart.

Tiger Lilies
burst into life
multiplying firebursts
grasping for sun

Scorched, I recoil
from John's favorite flowers
How can they bloom
If he is not here?

All the Stuff

There were so many practical matters to attend to, and grief was making it terribly difficult. Between the emotions, lack of sleep, and not eating well, my decision-making abilities took a real hit. For example, there were all of his possessions. What was I going to do with his stuff?

The first part of that was easy. It took about a year, but I decided to begin with his work clothes. John was a lawyer, and he wore suits and ties to the office for many years. He liked the work but hated the clothes. He never felt comfortable being dressed up, he was a shorts and t-shirt guy. So the first thing I got rid of were all of his suits, ties, and dress shirts. I donated them to charity, which felt good. The second thing I disposed of were his underwear and socks, which weren't invested with much emotion either, and could just be put in a big trash bag.

But when it came to other, more personal items, I froze. For a long time. I kept his toothbrush in the stand on the bathroom counter for several years.

My hand adjusts the faucet to a lukewarm temperature. I see my face in the mirror, lost, displaced. Who is that untethered person? That sad, isolated, middle-aged little girl? I lower my eyes to the counter and see his toothbrush, in its accustomed place next to mine.
His toothbrush.
He'd been to the dentist several times over the past year, endured cleanings and antibiotics and root canal and fitting for a new crown. I was so glad his breath had improved, it had been unpleasantly sour and embarrassing; when we were close I often stopped breathing to avoid the smell.
Straight, small teeth and a mischievous smile. Dimples, and eyes that shone with laughter or teasing amusement. Bellylaughs and chortles.
Cremated, he is only ash. He has no teeth, no dimples, no eyes, no throat, no belly. He has no anything. He is not. "He" does not exist.
No teeth to brush. I should get rid of that toothbrush. It is superfluous.
Everything is superfluous, my life is superfluous. There is no meaning, there is no reason, there is no use. I can throw away the toothbrush but I may as well throw away every damned item in this fucking house.
I take a shuddering breath, turn away from the sink, and leave the toothbrush where it is.

Every day I would look at it, ask myself if I could throw it out yet, and the answer was always no. Until, one day, it was yes. I threw it out, I cried, and it was done.

EVERYTHING CHANGED

Our house had been very cluttered, for many years. We were both pretty disorganized when it came to physical belongings, and like many people we had too much stuff we didn't use. After John died, I wondered if I should sell the house, changing my mind every month or so, swinging back and forth between wanting to move and make a fresh start and wanting to stay in our home, which was in a neighborhood I loved. Now that I lived alone, it meant I was solely responsible for deciding what was going to happen with all the stuff. And I knew that whether I stayed or moved, it was important for me to declutter and move out some of the stagnant energy. So, I planned to clean out every room of the house.

I thought beginning by decluttering in the kitchen would give me an easy start. After all, what's emotional about what's in the kitchen? It's pretty straightforward, stuff's either useful or not.

WRONG. I got stopped in my tracks a couple of times, and things haven't gone as quickly as I'd imagined they would. I didn't get weepy, but I got a terribly heavy sensation and had to walk away for a while. My body felt like it was carrying a huge load, and my brain just couldn't make a decision.

First, the tea cabinet. John's tea cabinet.

The good news – I didn't dissolve into tears. A couple of months, a few weeks ago, I probably would have. John's not here to drink tea anymore, waaah. He stopped drinking coffee and tried to drink healthful teas, a lot of good it did, waaah.

I had the thoughts and accompanying sadness, but not overwhelming grief.

But there was still the issue of what to do with it all. Man, he had a ton of stuff in there. All kinds of teas, most in packaging labeled in Chinese or Japanese. Some unopened, some opened, some not in original packaging. At least a dozen teas. And the teacups! The Chinese ones that have beautiful designs, with brewing inserts and lids. Ten or so of those. And little baby teacups, another half dozen. Another couple I had made for him in pottery class.

I had a difficult time deciding what to do with it all. I had to empty the shelves, leave everything on the kitchen counter, and walk away from it for a day. Then slowly sift through it.

His favorite Chinese teacup that he used most of the time had a broken lid. Into the trash it went. Most of the unopened tea was put aside – I'll give it to one of his tea-drinking friends. Some opened tea was tossed. And some was kept, put into a different cabinet – the one where I keep my coffee and teabags. The beautiful teacups were kept, put on a high shelf. I may have a tea party one day with those teacups and the lovely loose teas. Or I may give them as gifts.

Having cleaned out the cabinet, I've stocked it with casserole pans that I've begun using now that I'm cooking for myself again. They'd been stored on a higher shelf that was hard for me to reach. So it's nice to have transformed John's tea cabinet into a space to hold things I use on a weekly basis in the present.

It was surprisingly draining, this process. Distinguishing between what's past – John's broken teacup that I won't use, that's now discarded. What's present – well, nothing really because I don't drink those types of teas, but what to replace them with that serves me now. What's future possibility – perhaps I will prefer those types of teas someday. Perhaps I will have tea parties.

What's realistic, what's holding on. How I want to create my future, what's truly useful for that future, versus what's detritus from a past life that has ceased to exist.

Creating a future for myself that honors John and my life with him but doesn't hold me captive to my past. And it's so hard to let go of that past. I loved that life, I was robbed of it.

The second cabinet that threw me for a loop was the glasses cabinet. First shelf, coffee mugs and drinking glasses. Use them every day, no problem. Other shelves – wineglasses. Row after row of wineglasses. Wedding gifts. Chincoteague Oyster Festival beer mugs, too.

As a single woman, do I need to keep that many wineglasses? Should I give them all to charity? I almost never drink wine at home.

But in my future I would like to host dinner parties, in addition to tea parties. So for now I'm keeping all the wine glasses. They're on shelves I can't easily reach, anyway.

I didn't realize at the time that I was beginning to think about past, present, and future in ways that would wind up allowing me to find joy and live fully again. You'll read about that in Part 2 of this book, but first I had to get through the rest of my grief journey and find recovery.

I finally got to the point where I felt ready to go through the duffel bag he'd been travelling with on that last business trip. It sent me into a tailspin, reigniting the terrible anxiety that his death had triggered.

I've been trying, desperately, to become numb again. Flailing about, panicking, unmoored buffeted roiling. Lost. No bearing, no landmarks, no stars. No home.

I've lost my home. Home was where I was safe, but the illusion of safety has been shattered forever. And I spend every moment in fear, many of them in terror.

And it seems so lame. So ridiculous.

I lost someone I love. This is not an experience unique to me. It is the human condition. Life is ridiculously fragile, and people die every day. Husbands, wives, children, parents, friends, siblings. Every moment someone's loved one is dying.

How does the world keep spinning?

No, that's not the question.

How do people keep from spinning off into space?

I make small steps. Start to make progress on housecleaning. Get the briefest glimpse of the possibility of a future that is more than my grief. But then it all comes crashing down around me again.

What's completely crazy is that I didn't even realize how much I loved him when he was right here with me. I knew I loved him but I didn't know how epically. I didn't know I'd be nothing without him. How could I not have known?

Today I threw away his travel toiletry kit. The one he'd had with him on that last trip.

Toothpaste, toothbrush. For a smile I will never see again.

Diabetes test strips. For blood that doesn't flow.

Razor. For hair that does not grow.

Tylenol. He feels no pain. He feels nothing.

Soap.

A collapsible plastic cup. One I'd put in his Christmas stocking.

It has been 3 ½ years. Why do I still feel like the air's been knocked out of me? I still can't breathe. I still can't accept. I still want him here.

EVERYTHING CHANGED

I can't let go. I don't want to let go.

I don't want him to be just memories. I want to feel this hurt. It's as close as I can get to having a relationship with him.

And I struggled, a lot, with guilt over the fact that I wasn't there when he died.

I cannot be forgiven. You are not here to forgive me, and I cannot absolve myself.

How can I tell you that I'm sorry you died alone? How can I express the wrenching, churning horror of imagining how you felt? I am tortured.

I try to believe that you never knew it happened. That it was so massive an event it actually occurred without drama. A light switch, turned off.

This is what I want to believe:

You came home from your business trip, put down your duffel and backpack in the living room. Rasputin ran up to greet you, crying for his dinner. You were tired from the trip, from lugging the heavy bags the half mile from the train station. But happy to be home. Thinking about checking the mail, maybe turning on the TV.

You talked to Ras, walked into the kitchen. You didn't make it as far as opening the cabinet when *poof*.

You were gone.

You didn't know you fell, didn't feel pain, had no awareness anything had happened. Just poof and you were dead.

And it would have been no different had I been there.

This is what I fear:

You walked into the kitchen. Suddenly you felt great pain and your legs wouldn't support you. You fell on your back and were paralyzed. Lying there, terrified of what was happening, you tried like hell to move, to get up, to breathe, to live. But slowly, slowly, slowly, your heart stopped beating and you couldn't catch your breath. As Ras circled around you, you couldn't even speak to him, couldn't even turn your head. You wanted to cry out but there was no air. Your life flashed before your eyes. You were angry. So very angry. Wanting to curse God, but unable to speak or even to form words in your head. Cursing me for not being there with you, to help, to hold you, to tell you I love you.

How can I make amends for not being there? How can I give you all the love I feel, all the help you needed?

I need to tell you that I'm sorry. I'm sorry I wasn't with you at the end, to comfort and love and hold you. I should have been there for you. I should have been there.

I'm so sorry.

I'm sorry.

I'm sorry.

Most Surprising: Losing My Identity

This is the thing that shocked me: John dying made me feel like I didn't know who I was anymore.

We were not a couple who were joined at the hip. We each had interests and activities that the other didn't share. We'd met when I was 32 and had been living on my own for eight years. I considered myself an independent woman. We had an intimate emotional, physical, and intellectual relationship, but we spent a fair amount of time apart. If we were both at home, we were equally likely to be in separate rooms as we were to be interacting.

If you'd asked me, before, how I would feel if John died, I would have said I'd feel sad and lonely. But I never could have imagined how much I wouldn't feel like **myself** anymore. I no longer felt like Ellen. I felt like the widow, I felt like the person who was grieving, I felt like the person who was alone, I felt like a little girl who didn't know how to be a grownup, I felt like the person who is always and only sad, who is off-kilter, who is lost.

> *I don't know who I am without you*
> *I never knew how you changed me*
> *But without you I drift*
> *No center of gravity*
> *Why didn't I see*
> *Why didn't I know*
> *I loved you, yes*
> *I could have loved more*
> *I could have seen more*
> *I could have*
> *I didn't*
> *I can't*

One of the things that added to this sense of loss is the fact that I stopped working. When John was alive, I had a good job at a local university, where I worked in the communications department for development & alumni relations. I was writing, editing, proofreading, and managing a small team of excellent people. I loved my work. Six months after his death, there was a leadership change and I felt the need to leave, so I took on a similar role with my alma mater, a small liberal arts college. On paper, it was the perfect job for me. It was a new position, charged with creating a new program, and I had the exact right background and experience to bring to it. But my grieving brain couldn't do it. Although I did my best to appear "fine" to the world, inside I was still a mess. I wasn't sleeping, I couldn't think creatively, and I had trouble staying on task. So two years after I became a widow, I stopped working. I was fortunate that there was a generous life insurance policy that would allow me to take at least three years off, and I decided I would take that time to get over the grief. I did a little freelance work for my previous employer but decided I needed to redesign my life. Eventually, I was able to do that, as you'll see in Part 2. But first I had to go through some emotionally and intellectually uncertain years.

I left my job in December 2010. On January 1, 2011, this is what I wrote in my journal:

Starting to lay out a plan for this year, to begin to work on how to structure my time. This is what I wrote down:

> *Emotional*
>> *Space for feeling*
>> *Writing*
>> *Therapy*

Environment
> *Declutter, then clean, then improve (e.g., windows)*

Physical
> *Cooking/eating*
> *Gym*
> *Sleep*
> *Daily stretches*

Financial
> *Bills, savings, investing*

Intellectual
> *Reading – fiction + nonfiction*

Social
> *In-person, written correspondence, phone calls*

Spiritual
> *Meditation, music*

Artistic
> *Jewelry, pottery*

I look at that list and begin to cry. It's utterly overwhelming. How can I possibly begin even half the items on this list??

I know it's not an extraordinary list. People do all these things while working full time, while taking care of kids, having a family life.

But it feels extraordinary and out of my reach.

And that's when I realize it's not just my cognitive abilities that have suffered – it's my entire self.

I am broken, there are chunks of me missing.

And I'm terrified. Terrified that I won't be able to rebuild, that I'll never be whole again.

I realize I'm not just missing John, I'm missing me.

And then I realize I don't know how many of the pieces I've lost from grief, and how many I never had in the first place.

So now it feels utterly ridiculous to be trying to envision this life. It feels like a lie.

I would like to be the kind of person who could do all this. But I don't believe that I am.

Later that year, after a guided meditation, this is what I recorded of that experience:

I'm in a tunnel, with blue-gray walls, but it is circular, like I'm in a big tube. It seems endless, but then I see a small light in the distance. It feels like I could never reach the end, it's so far. And I'm afraid.

I take a deep breath and begin to walk, and then suddenly I am at the end of the tube.

Outside there is field and forest. I see someone approaching from a distance. I wait, afraid.

Is it? Could it be? Yes. John is walking toward me. Wearing jeans and a blue anorak, holding a walking stick. I walk toward him, try to catch his eye. He continues to come near but it's clear he doesn't see me.

Which one of us is real? We occupy the same space – I can see him, I take his hand – it's cool, unmoving – he doesn't grasp back.

I look at his face. He's not wearing his glasses. His eyes, I notice, are a much lighter shade of the color of the walls of my tunnel. His skin is mottled gray, from that night.

He walks, I follow. I want his attention but he can't see me, can't sense me. I need him to see me. I am not myself without him.

I don't know what's real anymore, I don't know who I am or what to do with my life.

What's the point? It's all gone.

I follow him. We come to a river and he looks out over the expanse. The sky is blue, the water flows. He will never be able to see me, to feel me. I cannot speak, I cannot reach him. He can't guide me anymore.

He climbs into a kayak and I watch as he paddles slowly away. He is at peace and I am in pieces. He has a destination and I am lost. He is gone and I am here.

What is the point?

He belongs in that world. I want to retreat back into my tunnel, to hide from a world that wants me to be alive, to do something, to be whole. I am bereft. I am a shadow. Who am I? What am I? What does it matter?

I am my grief. It is all that I am and all that I have.

The Invasive Vine of Grief

One part of identity that I lost was being the most important person in someone else's life. I am fortunate. I have parents, siblings, and good friends who are loving and supportive. People checked in on me. My brother called regularly to see how I was. My sister texted me multiple times a day, and still insists that I send her my agenda each week and let her know when I get home from different activities, which makes me feel safe and cared for. But none of that is quite the same as being someone else's point person, or having that partner you can just turn to and say that you heard about a new restaurant and we should try it for dinner, or knowing you'll always have a date for a wedding or someone to go to the movies with or to sit down at the dinner table with.

For a long time, I felt like I was failing John because I couldn't maintain his relationships with his family and friends. It sounds ridiculous now, but somehow I felt like I had a sacred obligation to fulfill his role as son, brother, friend. He couldn't do it so it was left to me. I even felt like I needed to experience and enjoy things he would have wanted to do, regardless of whether they appealed to me. It was a form of magical thinking, I suppose. It was almost as if I felt that I needed to maintain his life so that, if he ever came back, it would be there waiting for him. It's no wonder I lost my own identity, when I felt obligated to take his on instead.

Of course, I failed at that, too. I couldn't bring myself to do the things he liked that I hated, like watching horror movies or hiking or going camping in the winter. And I did a spectacularly lousy job of maintaining relationships with his family, whether as myself or on his behalf. I have great regrets about how difficult it was for me to interact with my mother-in-law because I couldn't handle her grief on top of my own; and she passed away a few years ago so now I'll never be able to reconnect or rebuild that relationship.

While I was going through all of this questioning, fear, loneliness, and anxiety, I did my very best to appear "fine" to others. Many grievers do this, and John W. James & Russell Friedman call it "Academy Award Recovery" in *The Grief Recovery Handbook*. It is difficult to know that you are seen as vulnerable, so I tried not to appear weak. Many people, actually, remarked on how strong I was and that they admired my strength – which made me want to scream, since it was all an act. No matter how strong I may have appeared, I was always a microsecond away from either exploding or fading away in my mind.

But the overwhelming reason I maintained my façade of "fine" was out of protectiveness. I knew that people loved me and worried about me and wanted me to be okay. I felt, truly felt, that I would never be okay again and that there wasn't anything that could be done about that. So, in order to protect those I love, I pretended. I know I wasn't totally successful, but I also know they didn't have any idea how bad it really was.

> *I have lost all sense of reality.*
> *My world has been destroyed*
> *but I'm sure it's all been a mistake*
> *and all will be restored.*
> *I saw, touched, tried to revive his corpse --*
> *and expect him to walk through the door.*
> *Disconnected from my own body, I observe it seeming to sleep,*
>   *eat, work, chat.*
> *I'm fine, thanks for asking.*

This was three and a half years after his death:

I am living a lie. Even though I have made so little progress on the outside, it's more than I've made on the inside.

I pretend that I want to move forward, that I want to accept and integrate this loss, that I want to live my life. But inside I'm still curled up in a ball with my eyes squeezed shut, trying desperately and fiercely to pretend none of this is real. I can't face a life without him. How did this happen? We weren't the type of couple who spent all our time together, who did all the same things, who depended on the other for company. I had absolutely no idea that we'd become so intimately and irreversibly intertwined. How can I go forth and be myself when I'm held back by him? I'm held back because the strands of his life are fused to the strands of mine. And he's stopped. He can't move forward. So I can strain to take a step, but I'm held fast by his nonmovement.

When he was alive, the strands were intertwined, but they were elastic. I moved in one direction, he moved in another, the strands stretched and moved and kept us connected so that we always came back together. He became more me and I became more him. But when he died, I tried to keep him with me by wrapping myself tightly in his strands. The strands are now like rope or wire, keeping me where I am. There's no give anymore. They limit me but they protect me. Protect me from a world in which he no longer exists.

He died, but I have become a ghost. This façade walks through the world, performing tasks, socializing, breathing, eating. But just behind the screen I am in shadow, eyes closed and brain numb. Moving neither through life nor time, drifting in pain and loneliness.

Riding the Waves

Let me clarify something: I had good days. I had plenty of days when I felt okay, when I believed my life would be meaningful again, when I felt I was making progress toward recovery. But grief is like the ocean, it comes in waves. Some lap at your legs, some crash into your chest, some knock you off your feet. They're unpredictable. Sometimes you can see them coming, but sometimes they sneak up on you. And you never know how much time there will be between them. Sometimes they come one after another, boom boom boom. Sometimes you think they're over, you think you're done, you think it will remain placid – and you're wrong. And when they knock you down and hold you underwater, it feels like it will always be that way.

Here is my description of the waves of grief, as experienced after a guided meditation. The beginning of the story is an actual childhood memory.

The beach. Bright sun, warm breeze. The briny scent of the ocean mixed with tropical cocoa butter slippery on my skin.

We have been building sandcastles, using water to make the sand clump into tower-making cement. A moat to protect the princess who lives inside.

How old am I? Four or five. My sister, seven or eight, takes my hand as we wade into the water to jump over the waves. My feet step gingerly on broken shells. There are mysteries here.

My parents must be watching over us but I am only aware of the ocean, the wind, and my sister's hand in mine. She is sure of herself. I am scared but in a good, excited way. This is new, this is daring.

The water is warm. It laps up my calves, the bottom of my bathing suit gets damp. Small ripples come, Barb holds my hand more tightly as she guides me to ride the rolling, massaging smoothness passing below. We jump as the water peaks and it is like flying. I am a mermaid, transformed.

Free, laughing, spirit flying.

Wham!

My feet are no longer under me. My hands are empty. I am floating, engulfed by salt water. But the water is warm, I have instinctively held my breath, all is fine. I go to stand and shake my wet head...

I am trapped. Face down, under water, the wave is passing over and its force keeps me down. For a second or two. Forever.

Shocked, I try harder to move but am paralyzed. I will never arise, I will be floating under water for the rest of my life. I will die here.

The eternal moment passes, the wave recedes, and I am fine. Barbara is right there, I can breathe, I can walk, we go back to our beach towels and family. Life continues.

I am trapped again, beneath waves of grief. They come without warning, some low, some high. Warm, cold, sharp, perpetual. Shocking and expected.

I move through my days, performing tasks, enjoying friends or music or video games. Moving forward. Until I am knocked over suddenly and can't breathe, can't move, can't live without him.

I am learning. Ride out the wave. The harder you fight the more futile your effort. Give in. It will pass and you will float to the surface again.

Until next time.

CHAPTER 2

Clueless and Searching

Widowhood is a Detour. Where's My GPS?

I have a terrible sense of direction. I come by it naturally, as my mother is the same way. My sister has said that I have as much sense of direction as a dead moose! My husband coined the perfect term – he said that I am geodyslexic. I am grateful beyond words for the advent of GPS, because for many years I hated to drive if I didn't know for sure how to get where I was going, irrationally terrified that I would wind up so lost I would never be able to find my way home again.

Well, widowhood for me was like driving on a strange road. I didn't know where I was, I couldn't find any street signs, and I didn't even know what my destination was. It was dark and rainy and I couldn't see the lines to be sure I was in the correct lane. For me, that's a scene from my personal horror movie.

For the first year, I felt I was walking through a blinding snowstorm, buffeted by winds. Wet and cold, then numb, not sure how I could continue to put one foot forward. My brain felt like a frozen block of ice.

Then, in the second year, things started to thaw a bit – which made each day even harder. No longer frozen, I began to really feel all of the despair, fear, and loneliness. My brain wasn't a block of ice anymore, it was Swiss cheese that had been left out in the sun, riddled with holes and melting at the edges.

This is my journal entry as the first anniversary of his death approached and the second year began:

I'm starting to relive that awful, awful night. But this time I'm really feeling it. Last year, when it actually happened – WHEN JOHN DIED – I immediately went into shock mode I guess. I do know that as soon as I began to think it wasn't a joke and picked up the phone to call 911, I separated. I knew I couldn't panic, that I had to hold it together. So I did. And I called 911 and I tried to resuscitate him and I called Lisa and I called Barb and Mom and Dad and Rob ... And I made a funeral home decision and I guess I fed Rasputin? And all along I felt like I was watching myself, or that I was playing a character in someone else's life. It wasn't real, it couldn't be real.

Now it feels real. And it feels terrifying and horrible. And I'm not only remembering all of those things I had to do, but I'm really feeling it now. It's my life, not someone else's. It's not a dream, not a movie, not an alternate universe.

It almost sent me to my knees in the shower this morning.

I was nervous almost all the time with a general, unfocused, on-the-verge-of-a-panic-attack anxiety. I spent a lot of time fighting the urge to scream, then feeling overwhelmingly tired and completely without energy. It was a struggle simply to get out of bed. And through it all, my brain just couldn't accept that he was never coming back. It's not that I was in denial about his death, it was that I couldn't imagine continuing to live the rest of my life without him there.

Going Through the Motions and Losing Time

I felt like I was inhabiting a surreal world. It felt fictional, like watching myself in a dream or as if I somehow had ended up in the wrong universe. My emotions and reactions bobbled and jumped around from year to year, month to month, day to day. You'll see throughout my recollections that the chronology seems off kilter.

Every day, I expected it all to be a nightmare, that I would finally wake up and be in the reality I was supposed to be living in, the one where I had my husband beside me.

Time became bizarre, fluid, elastic, loopy, unreal, unpredictable, stretching and collapsing. I felt he'd been gone forever, and at the same time it felt as if it had happened a moment ago, and time just didn't feel linear anymore.

It just hit me that John has been gone – dead – for more than 2 ½ years. Obviously, I knew that, but it's like I just realized how long 2 ½ years is.

How is it possible that I have lived without him for this long? How can it be that far in the past, when the pain is still so immediate, so all-consuming, so constant?

It's weird. It doesn't feel like it's been that long. Shouldn't it feel like it's been longer, like it's been forever? But no, it feels like it's all new and raw and unstable. I suppose when you're drifting through the days, meandering through the rubble of what was once your life, not grounded, trying not to feel too much, because if you feel everything you will combust – that in a way you're not experiencing all of those days that become 2 ½ years.

Two and a half years is longer than our pre-engagement dating life. Hell, it's longer than the time between our meeting and our wedding.

How is it possible that time has kept going? How is it possible that everybody else has lived over 2 ½ years of their lives while I've only seen shadows?

I felt like I was moving through jello. Sometimes I felt like I was going to stop and not remember how to move, or breathe. I was weighed down, as if there were rocks in my pockets, in my shoes, in my soul. I knew I had to work, that there were things that needed to get done, but I couldn't focus, couldn't care. I just wanted to curl up in fetal position and fade away. John felt just out of reach – like if I just tried a little harder or were a little cleverer or a little stronger, I could reach out and touch his hand again.

I guess the key – or one of the keys – is to try not to focus on the future, which is overwhelmingly empty without him. Just get through the day. One step at a time, one breath at a time. But everything is so damned heavy. My body, the air, gravity. I can't fight gravity anymore. It's pushing me down, pulling me down. Down. And I don't have the energy to rise above.

CLUELESS AND SEARCHING

Weighted
Pulled down
Encumbered
This body, this brain, this heart
Torpid
Inert
Dull
How can I breathe in a vacuum? How can I move through rubber cement?
Imploding, sagging, I sink into the abyss

I had "good" days, too. Days when I wasn't happy, but I was okay. Days when it felt like I could do this, I could one day be happy again even if I weren't happy now. Days when I found pleasure in being with friends or seeing a play or listening to music. But the grief continued to come in unpredictable waves. Usually, if I'd had a few okay days in a row, and would get lulled into believing that I was getting over the loss, a huge wave of grief would come knock me on my butt and make me want to keep the covers pulled up over my head again. It was never a straight path toward feeling better.

I felt like I'd been sitting and watching a movie ever since he'd died. Some parts were more engaging than others, but mostly it was just ... there. I was ready for the movie to be over. I wanted to stand up, leave the theater, and walk blinking out in the sunlight to return to the life I was SUPPOSED to be living, the one where I go home and my husband has made a pot of chili or his delicious African chicken stew. Where we plan the menu for Thanksgiving. Where we decide what we're buying everyone for Christmas/Hanukkah. Where he annoys me by playing loud music I don't like, or doesn't wipe up a spill. Where he and I sit down to watch TV together and nitpick about the good and bad. Where we go to sleep, and I get a hot flash and don't want him snuggling next to me because the last thing I need to feel is his body heat.

Working Through Grief

Looking back, it seems absurd that I ever thought I'd be able to be a competent employee in the first years after John died. I think that, had I been able to stay at the job I'd been in for the last ten years, then I would have done well enough. I knew the work so well that I could do a portion of it almost on autopilot; I had a terrific team who could have, and would have, picked up the slack; I had caring bosses who would have given me as much support as possible. The familiar surroundings and friends I had there would have provided structure that made me feel more myself, at least while I was at the office.

But that's not how it worked out. A change in leadership created an atmosphere of competition and frenetic uncertainty, and the last thing I needed in my life was additional stress. But taking a new job, at a different organization, didn't work out well either. I simply could not muster the creative thinking to build a new program, even though my skills and experience should have made it easy for me. But when you're walking through gelatin and barely able to get out of bed and feeling like you're not even really inhabiting your life, you can't be expected to learn and grow. My bosses were kind and understanding, and they gave me as much flexibility as they could. But my brain was melting Swiss cheese, and it wasn't processing as it should.

There were so many days when I felt queasy. So anxious, so sad. I felt like my heart was about to jump out of my chest. My throat was tight, my limbs were vibrating, someone was squeezing my head. I couldn't focus, I couldn't concentrate. I was probably only able to give about 20% of myself to the job.

I struggled with making decisions about my life. I felt the need to take time off but wasn't sure it was the right thing to do. I needed my main source of support to help me make those decisions, but he was dead. John was always in my corner. And now the corner was empty. Nobody else could fill that same role. I felt all alone, and scared.

In addition to my lack of mental acuity, I started getting sick. The lack of sleep, stress, poor eating habits, and sedentary lifestyle I'd been indulging in caught up to me. It started a little over a year past his death – despite having gotten the flu vaccine, I came down with two different strains of the flu. I got a stomach virus. And I developed shingles.

I was extraordinarily fortunate in being able to afford to stop working for a few years. Thanks to savings and life insurance, I could stay home and focus on processing my emotions. I could indulge my desire to sleep all day. I could hibernate. But all of that may have contributed to my continuing depression.

I had lost my love for life. I never felt suicidal, but I had no interest in living. I felt as though I were simply marking time, getting through each day so I could be closer to the time I wouldn't have to bother to try anymore.

Monumental, Mundane Adjustments

Everything about my life had changed, and everything needed to be adjusted. Simple things took on ridiculously meaningful significance.

Like most couples, John and I had divided the household tasks. One thing he was solely responsible for was taking the trash to the curb every week. Now, every single Wednesday I struggled with fury as I put out the garbage. Each time it was a stark reminder that I was alone, that he was no longer with me, that my life wasn't the one I wanted anymore.

Choosing recipes to cook became a minefield. I found myself skipping over dishes that sounded delicious to me but were things I knew wouldn't be to his taste. Similarly, I gravitated to meals that he would have loved but weren't really my preference – then the realization that he wasn't there to enjoy it would come crashing down around my ears again. I started thinking I had to only cook things he wouldn't have liked, because it would be a shame to make anything he'd enjoy since he wasn't there to eat it. Even at the time, I realized I was being irrational, but that didn't stop the thoughts from coming.

Beautiful days made me sad.

Too many dreary days depressed me, but lovely sunny breezy days made me sad for John, that he wasn't here to enjoy them. I couldn't distinguish how much of my sadness was for me, missing him and how much was for him, missing out on this world. I was filled with regret for everything he was missing, for everything he would never have the chance to do now. And I was angry with him for the things he had put off doing.

Figuring Out Self-care

Despite all my emotions and the fact that I felt like I was watching my life instead of living it, I instinctively knew I needed to take care of myself. I knew I couldn't just stay in bed with the covers pulled over my head (at least not every day), I knew that wouldn't lead me to anything positive or bring me back to life.

I struggled mightily with balance: how much "doing" is too much, how much is too little? As a natural introvert but a social person who loves her friends, I questioned myself constantly. I knew I needed to have time alone to journal and to sleep and to be alone, because that felt like self-preservation. But I also knew that could easily slip into wallowing and worsen my depression.

My best friend, Lisa, was the person who helped me the most with this. She knows me well and had a keen instinct for understanding when I needed to be left alone and when I needed prodding to get out of the house. Especially in the very early days, it was she who kept me going, got me a little fresh air, kept me from hiding away completely. I will be forever grateful.

As time went on, three things kept me grounded and connected to the world of the living.

I love dogs, but I am a cat person at heart. When we got married, I had three cats and John had two. I often joke that we had a blended family, and called them "The Brady Cats," referring to the 1970s television program *The Brady Bunch*. At the time of his death, there was only one cat left in the house. His name was Rasputin; he was an orange tabby who had been one of John's original pets and was the sweetest cat I've ever known. He was very old, and four months after John died, he passed away – on what happened to be John's birthday. That was a very hard day for me.

My first instinct was to wait a while before adopting a new cat, since I hadn't decided yet whether I was going to keep our house or move. But after living completely alone for two weeks I realized I needed someone to talk to! I went to a local rescue organization and found a sweet three-year old gray cat named Hope. Hope! That was exactly what I needed in my life. She has been a loving, wonderful companion.

Having first Rasputin, then Hope, to care for was important. Needing to feed them and clean the litter box, and having them to interact with, gave me a reason to get out of bed every morning.

I do have good friends, and many of them are single women. I was very fortunate not to have lost my main source of social interaction when John died. So many widows, who have socialized mainly as couples with other couples, find they are the "odd woman out" once their husbands pass away. That wasn't my situation – and having those lunches and dinners, and previously purchased theater and concert ticket subscriptions, made me get up and out of the house periodically. Even on the occasions when I wasn't totally "there" emotionally or mentally, they gave me stimulation beyond the walls of my house.

Although I left my long-held job seven months after John died, and only stayed at the new one for a year and a half, they were important for keeping me grounded, too. I wasn't very productive, and I called in sick often, and wound up having to leave because I couldn't handle the demands of work, but even so I think it was good for me to have someplace to be. As long as I was working, I was getting fresh air on my commute and I was thinking about something other than being a widow for at least a few minutes or hours each day.

Menopause + Grief = Anxiety

I suffered with tremendous anxiety after John died, something I hadn't experienced before. I felt unsafe and insecure, and exposed. I had terrible trouble sleeping. About a year after his death I started to need to leave the lights on, which made me feel weak. My therapist explained that it wasn't a weakness, it was a coping strategy. And, if I gave myself permission to do it, then I wouldn't feel as if I were failing. That did work, and I began to turn off the bedroom lights but leave the bathroom light on so I wasn't plunged into total darkness right before going to sleep. It helped, but I still had a generalized anxiety I couldn't shake.

I spoke to my doctor about it, and he prescribed a low dose of antidepressants. That helped me a bit, but for someone who is already feeling sometimes like she's divorced from her real life it probably wasn't the best treatment, as I was still feeling my emotions but they were blunted, like I couldn't quite get at them. I took the pills for six months but decided to stop (under my physician's guidance) after that. I think I might have fared better with an anti-anxiety medication or a sleep aid.

After I stopped taking the antidepressants, I slowly began to notice something important about my anxiety. It so happened that I was going through menopause at the same time I was grieving my husband's death. One day I had the realization that the feeling I was identifying as anxiety – a tight feeling in my abdomen accompanied by a general mild tingling in my arms and legs – almost always preceded a hot flash. And once the hot flash was over, that anxious feeling would fade as well.

Before I made that connection, the feeling would wash over me, and immediately my mind would start to think, "I feel anxious. What do I have to be anxious about?" And I came up with lots of reasons, some of them very creative. "A tree could fall on the house. The furnace could explode. Maybe the oven was left on. I don't know if I have enough money." It went on and on, and thinking of those things only increased my stressed-out mental state.

Now, when I start to feel my stomach tighten up, I stop and breathe. "Are you anxious, or is it a hot flash?" I wait a minute, and begin to feel the heat rise through my body and the anxiety recede. Understanding what was happening in my body, and that it was a physical rather than an emotional reaction, was an important factor in my self-care.

CHAPTER 3

Our Relationship

Why Did We Become Us?

Who was this man, who meant so much to me that his death shattered my world into a billion pieces? He was passionate, angry, funny, frustrated, sweet, irreverent, romantic, and fair-minded.

At first glance, you wouldn't think we belonged together. He listened to punk and thrash, I prefer pop and show tunes. He loved horror movies and books, I like romantic comedies and literary fiction. He loved kayaking, hiking, and hunting for fossils, while I love the theater, choral singing, and being cozy at home with a cup of hot chocolate.

He was a pessimist. I am an optimist. He saw the sleazy underbelly of the world, while I saw the light and love. Together, we averaged out to a pretty realistic view of things.

We both liked science fiction, classic rock, and Celtic music. We both loved cats and treated them not like children, but as full-fledged feline members of our family. We shared a belief in the importance of trust, loyalty, and honesty. We balanced each other.

He taught me patience. I had been terribly impatient my entire life. But I found that because he was impatient, too, I needed to find more equanimity to cancel that out.

Similarly, he taught me to control my temper. We were both very quick to anger. If I'd continued to lose mine as often as he did his, we'd both be angry all the time. So I learned to breathe more, to let a little more roll off my back. I couldn't control his reactions, so I had to control mine.

He broadened my humor horizon. I'd been relatively prim regarding what I found funny, but now I can see the humor in things a bit more vulgar and irreverent than I used to: The Three Stooges, South Park, The Simpsons. I wouldn't have found them so amusing, but he helped me break down some of my prissiness so I could see the cleverness and not be turned off by the shock value.

He also gave me more to enjoy in speculative fiction. I'd always loved some forms of sci-fi, but with him I felt safe enough to be able to handle the distress of things a little scarier – we loved to watch *The X-Files* together, but without him I think the monster aspect of those stories would have made me turn off the TV. No, I never got to a point where I liked true horror or things that got too gory. But I was exposed to more, and my threshold for what I could handle was raised.

The greatest gift I think he gave me was a belief in my own creative, artistic abilities. I'd once bought a child's craft kit, on a whim, of some beads – and he saw that and ran with the concept.

On my next birthday, he gave me a completely unexpected gift: a set of beads and findings. Crystals, seed beads, spacers, clasps, ear wires, and some basic tools. I was floored. And I felt just like a little kid with a bright shiny toy. I still wear some of the first earrings I made with that. And it wasn't a kit someone else had put together – he chose every item, all the pretty colors and interesting shapes.

I'd spent most of my life, up to that point, believing that I wasn't artistic or creative. With that gift, he blew away that concept. He believed in me. He let me bring back a huge part of myself I hadn't realized had been exiled since childhood.

Because of that gift, I began to make jewelry. I began to make my own polymer clay beads. I *sold* my jewelry. There, too, he was wonderful. When I decided to participate in a local craft fair, he was my roadie. He helped me transport and set up, and he kept me company. And he wasn't as surprised as I by how much I sold. What a fabulous, affirming feeling, to have strangers pay money for things I created! He very tangibly and concretely supported me in following my dreams. His love and belief unblocked me.

Our First Date

We met on a blind date. It didn't take long to see that we enjoyed each other's conversation and that he was a romantic at heart.

He calls me on the phone, at work. It is two days after our blind date. Casual – how are you? Would you like to have lunch sometime?

It is mid-February. The fourteenth is this week. I answer, airy – how about Tuesday, or Thursday? He chooses Thursday. I wonder, does he know that's Valentine's Day?

We'd had such a nice dinner. I hadn't even known I had a checklist in my head regarding my ideal mate, but as we'd talked I found myself ticking off items: smart, check. Funny, check. Animal lover, check. Science fiction fan, check. Articulate, check. Plus that feeling – that he was considerate, loyal, sweet. We felt comfortable enough with each other to discuss cat litter over dinner: clay or clumping?

Afterward, he sent me a note. And Belgian chocolates! This guy could be a keeper.

I was excited about this. I'd given up on meeting the right guy; resigned myself to finding happiness as a single woman. But this man was special – maybe.

Thursday arrived. I dressed with special care – don't look like you're trying too hard but wear something especially flattering. The morning raced by; the morning wouldn't end.

Noon. We meet outside the restaurant, a few blocks away from both our buildings. He's wearing a suit, an overcoat. Carrying a large black umbrella on this misty day.

We sit, we eat, we talk. I like him as much as I'd thought I did! This could really be the start of something. Something big. (Don't get ahead of yourself, don't make it more than it is.) He's someone I'd like to know better. I hope this goes somewhere. I hope he feels the same.

Although it's in the opposite direction from his office, he walks me back to mine. The skies threaten, but the rain is holding off for now. We pause outside the building, and he asks me out for Saturday night. We linger on the sidewalk another minute or two. Just as I'm about to go inside, he pulls one long-stemmed red rose from the closed umbrella. "Happy Valentine's Day."

We were close to inseparable from then on. Our first "real" date, after the blind date and then our lunch on Valentine's Day, happened to be the long President's Day weekend – and we wound up spending all three days and nights together.

The First of Many Birthday Extravaganzas

My birthday is in February, his was in March. Every year, we did more and more to honor each occasion, stretching the celebrations over several days. We called it the "birthday extravaganza."

A month after we met, we had our first extravaganza when we went to a bed & breakfast for the weekend to celebrate his birthday.

We had a picnic, we browsed in a used book store, and we went to a state park to fly kites. He was so happy – we were so happy! I was already in love with him. Carefree. It was the first spring weather weekend, with a bright blue sky and green buds on the trees and a warm sun and cool breeze, and I felt light and free and beautiful and joyful. He taught me to fly the kite, he was patient and I didn't feel stupid for not knowing how. Our connection grew so deep so quickly, but it was completely natural and right.

Summers with Ponies

We used to spend a week every summer in Chincoteague, Virginia. Chincoteague is far from a one-horse town, what with all the wild ponies, but it is small and contained. Every year we would rent a big house, and host friends and family.

We walked on the beach and wildlife trails, looking for the beautiful ponies, deer, turtles, and birds: blue herons, and the "long-necks", as we called the ibises. I remember once coming across a chestnut mare and her very young foal the color of barely toasted marshmallows, who was lying down on his side just off the path. I worried he was sick, but as we stood and watched he lurched to his feet on the long unwieldy legs he was just learning to use and they walked off together. It seemed as though he'd just gotten so tired all of a sudden that he'd had to plop down right there for a few minutes.

John and the gang always went on one or two day-long hikes and paddles. I stayed back at the house at those times, feeling inadequately unathletic.

I curled up with a book, I made jewelry from my polymer clay beads, I shopped in the quaint stores on Main Street. It was my vacation too and I had a right to do what relaxed *me* – but it made me wonder how I'd fallen in with this active, outdoorsy family.

One year, at the last moment, I couldn't go on our usual vacation. One of the cats was sick and I needed to stay with her, comfort and medicate her. Ironically, the cottage we had leased that season was called Kateague. Of course, because we'd invited other people to share our rental house, one of us – John – needed to go as planned.

About six weeks later, John insisted that he had to make it up to me, that it wasn't right that I had to miss out on my Chincoteague experience that summer. We rented a hotel room and we drove down in the quiet days after Labor Day, just the two of us. He was still working at the law firm then and was called back to the office after just one day. I stayed while he drove the four hours back, dealt with the work issue, then returned two days later. As it happened, it rained almost the entire time he was gone so I didn't have much to keep myself entertained. But TNT was running a marathon, and that was when I first got hooked on *Law & Order* reruns.

When John came back we had a couple of lovely slow days together. On our last evening, close to sundown, we drove around the Wildlife Loop on the Assateague National Wildlife Refuge. Suddenly, we found ourselves surrounded by a swarm of dragonflies! Swooping, swirling, iridescent green, pink, and gold fairies filled the sky. We sat, transfixed, smiling in wonder at each other. It was a moment to remember.

International Travel

We took three big trips together in addition to our honeymoon on St. John in the US Virgin Islands. We spent a week driving around Nova Scotia; he made up silly songs and poems about us in the car. We went to China and saw amazing things. There are so many memories from those vacations, but this is the one I want to share. It's from the time we travelled to Oaxaca, Mexico with an alumni group from my college.

The streets are narrow and tangled, the houses not much more than painted shacks.

We have been brought here to see the artists and their work – these people who, in their humble surroundings, carve fantastical animals, bringing life back to the dead wood. Adding detachable limbs, wings, tails, and painting them with vibrant colors in psychedelic patterns that swirl.

The trip has been a good one, once we got past the actual travelling part of getting to the airport, through security, to the gate. John, as always, anxious and afraid of flying – and being a pain in the ass about it. The sole purpose of every other person there was to be in his way. Impatient and snappy, he ensured I would be tense as well.

But now we are deep into the week in Oaxaca. We have gone to the market and sipped spicy, cinnamon-spiked hot chocolate. We have seen potters at work – in the factory where they make the shiny black vessels, and in the backyards where an old woman uses clay to fashion hoochie girls with full breasts barely contained by green sparkly dresses.

Today we go from house to house, buying and buying so many wonderful wooden critters, lizards and alligators, unicorns, penguins, dragons, and giraffes. The exchange rate makes it easy to overindulge. We have been told to haggle, to get the best deal. But on our first day in Mexico John told me he doesn't feel comfortable doing that here – he says it's ridiculous to get the seller down to a price that means the difference of a dollar or two to us, but perhaps a day's groceries to them. So we just pick up all we want, and pay what is asked.

At the last house, we admire a large jaguar. It's huge – three times the size of the other things we've seen. Rather than the riot of colors we've seen on the painted pieces, this has been left raw, polished brown wood. It gleams. It is magnificent.

Another couple in our group has already claimed it, and we are disappointed.

The son of the artist, a boy of 13 or so, indicates in broken English that we should wait here. He disappears into the workshop that is also his home and returns with a few more carvings, including a large turtle and another jaguar. It is half the size of the other, and painted in stripes and triangles and circles of teal, black, red, and yellow. The mouth is wide open, the fangs are bright white.

John asks the boy if he is the one who made these, and the answer is yes. We admire them and offer to buy this jaguar, without bargaining. The boy is beaming with pride, it is the biggest sale he has ever made.

We assure him that we love it, it is beautiful, and it will have a place of honor in our home.

John loved that piece, both for its beauty and because it held the memory of that young man and his first forays into the world of adulthood and success as an artist.

It watches over me from atop the fireplace mantel in the living room, protecting me from evil spirits and reminding me of my cranky but kindhearted husband's generosity of spirit.

Halloween

I have many special memories from our seventeen years together, and could fill an entire book with all of them.

I warm my hands on the mug of cider, breathing in the sweet, spicy vapors. Taking a sip, I taste apples, cinnamon, cloves, orange. John has his own cup, of sugar-free Swiss Miss hot chocolate. He doesn't even notice the taste of artificial sweeteners that I find cloying and bitter.

We are huddled in our jackets, listening to the sounds of costumed children on the sidewalks. The candles in our jack o'lanterns glow, bringing to mind Linus and his Great Pumpkin.

I'd never carved a pumpkin before. John showed me how to slice off the top with a sharp knife then scoop out the stringy innards and seeds, scraping the sides to get out all the goop. We each made our own, easy to distinguish. His, of course, was meant to be scary – a demon, a monster. Grimaced and evil. Mine, of course, was a cat, a witch's familiar. Magical, powerful, and love personified.

The real cats were inside the house. If we'd opened the door every time the children came we would have been trying to put candy in bags through the tiniest opening possible while body- and foot-checking anyone trying to get out. In reality, as soon as the doorbell rang they probably would have all scattered, frightened by that piercingly loud bell. But we didn't think it was worth taking chances.

Besides, we enjoyed sitting out of the porch together, remembering holidays past. Exchanging stories of costumes. John's had been homemade, sewn by his mother for him and his brothers. They'd been dragons, astronauts. I usually had a store-bought outfit, exciting in its newness. The smell of vinyl, the slippery smoothness of the cape, the hard plastic mask making my face sweat. Such an innocent, trusting time – small children ringing every doorbell, no concern for whether we knew who lived there. Playing, for an hour or two, a brave character, a strong character, fantastical, beautiful, frightening.

We sit companionably, we've talked in quiet voices about our days, shared annoyances of work and commute. On our porch, with our lighted pumpkins, we feel the excitement of the night. A night of mystery, magic, fear, transformation.

We can see dark shapes of ghosts, ballerinas, Jedi knights, superheroes as they travel in packs with flashlights. Only a few come to our house – we live on a small block between two major roads, and most trick-or-treaters skip it. Not worth turning the corner for these seven properties when there are more houses with greater treasure to be had by going straight down the avenue. Little do they know we have Snickers, Reese's, Kit Kats galore. The few who do venture here go laden with handfuls of chocolate.

No matter. The real magic of the night is sitting quietly together, as the sweet liquids warm our bodies and the time together warms our spirits.

Thanksgiving

We loved Halloween, but Thanksgiving was our favorite holiday.

Thanksgiving has always been one of my favorite holidays. I love that it's about counting one's blessings, appreciating family, and enjoying delicious food. No presents to buy, no decorations. Just a feast to say "we are grateful for what we have, and for the people we love." And it's a holiday for everyone, not just people who believe a certain something or other. It's inclusive.

It's always been a pretty intimate holiday for my family. Mostly just us, the immediate family, with a few folks invited here or there – a college friend too far from home to travel for the weekend, an elderly great-aunt and her nurse companion, a favorite aunt and uncle. Low-key and easy does it.

I remember waking up, as a kid, to the savory aroma permeating the house of the turkey beginning to roast. It made me feel warm and protected and relaxed. And hungry.

My parents had just begun going down to Florida for the winter. The worst thing about that would have been not having our traditional Thanksgiving. I certainly didn't have the first idea how to cook such a meal. But that's where you saved us. You had no hesitation about cooking a turkey, and had experience doing it.

The feasts you prepared! Every year, adding more side dishes. I think we were up to 13 of them! Herbed bread stuffing, mashed potatoes, roasted sweet potatoes with crystallized ginger, mashed turnips, creamed onions, Brussels sprouts, string beans with almonds, I can't even name them all. The table, even with both spare leaves, could barely hold the food. We all loved it.

Do you remember the first year? We moved into our new house in September, got married in October, and hosted Thanksgiving in November. We didn't even have a dining room table yet – we set up a folding aluminum table in the dining room. We rushed to get our new living room furniture delivered. We had that huge open space with a cathedral ceiling and fireplace. We got a couch, loveseat, and chairs just in time.

I love that you were so hospitable. That was something we shared – the desire to make our guests comfortable and relaxed. That's mostly why we always had food in such quantity. No one should feel as if someone else might go without as many servings as they'd like. The food shouldn't look as if it were running out, ever. And it never did. We sent guests home with containers of leftovers and still had plenty for us, so we could all continue to enjoy the feast for days.

And then you died. You died on the Friday before Thanksgiving. My favorite holiday is now empty, hollow, tasteless.

Vermont

John grew up in New Jersey, but his mother and stepfather lived in Vermont, and we used to visit a least a couple of times a year.

Jumbled images. Vermont. Visits to the farm.

It is Christmas. The tree fills the room with a sharp piney smell.

It is summer. We go swimming in the pond, kicking up mud, watching dragonflies glide.

The mountains are green and lavender, the air sweet. The tall hay waves in the wind.

OUR RELATIONSHIP

The streets are treacherously icy. The wind howls and the wood stove is cozy.

This is his mother's home. Not the house he grew up in but one that he loved. I can't remember the whole of any one visit. It saddens and scares me that I cannot.

It comes down to this: I have never had a detailed memory. Friends will tell stories of our youth, that we went here and did that, and this one said this and that one responded.

My memories are all of feelings. I know how I reacted or what I felt but I don't usually remember scenarios, conversations, chronology.

And now my memories, my incomplete blurred memories, are all I have left of him.

I have snatches, snapshots in my mind, emotions like love and anger and bemusement and frustration and happiness ... but I don't have the stories.

He was the storyteller. He remembered everything, he was my historian. The stories he told, over and over, the ones I stopped listening to because I'd heard them so many times – I can't remember the stories.

If I can't tell his story, our story, how can I remember him? If I can't tell his story he will never have existed. But how can I tell his story without plot? Without dialogue? Without characters?

What is the truth of his story? Of our story? The truth is, he was here and I am different because I knew him.

The truth is he gave me the love and support that allowed me to discover my creative side, he introduced me to silly humor, he taught me what to do in case of a zombie attack ... and there's more, I know there's so much more. If only I could remember.

Playing Hearts at the kitchen table. Barbecuing on the deck. Spotting a moose in the tall grass. Opening presents, exploring the barn. Snapshots of Vermont.

In the years since I wrote that in my journal, more memories have emerged. But it's true that I remember less of the narrative of our lives, and more of the feelings. And that's okay. I've not only made my peace with it, I embrace it. Because the feelings are what truly matter.

CHAPTER 4

Isolation: Motives and Methods

Alone in a Crowd

I've already said that I have been fortunate, in that I have loving, caring family members and friends who did what they could to care for me in my grief. They checked in on me. They invited me out. In some cases, they *insisted* I come out, if only for fifteen minutes.

Some grievers have a very different experience. Some people are very uncomfortable observing grief, so they exhort their friend or loved one to "get over it" or "keep busy" or hide their feelings in some way. That didn't happen to me. Nobody told me I should stop talking about John. Nobody dismissed my feelings.

And yet, I isolated myself.

This happens to the majority of grievers, and it's one of the worst things they can do. Connection is what keeps us strong, love and friendship is at the core meaning of our lives. But grievers separate. Why?

Some, as I've said, do it because they don't get support. Some do it because the pain of grief is so distressing that they begin to disconnect themselves from their other relationships – they don't want to experience that hurt again should someone else in their lives die or leave. Some do it because they feel too uncomfortable showing vulnerability. Some do it because they seek to protect those they love from knowing just how devastated they really are.

At Work

I found it very difficult to work. Of course, I wanted to be perceived, as I always had been, as competent, mature, in control. And I felt like I was none of those things anymore. So in order to hide my vulnerability I shut myself in my office, behind a computer screen, with a mind that refused to focus and a heart that was broken.

I am sitting across from my boss, a woman my age who until recently was one of my coworkers. She is lecturing me. I nod. I respond, a bit. I act as if I am anxious, and eager, to please her, to be the employee she wants me to be.

What she doesn't realize is that I am not even in the room anymore, that she is talking to a shell, a statue. A ghost.

She talks about my "difficult situation." The best way for me to move forward after the sudden and unexpected death of my husband a few months earlier is to throw myself into my work. After all, her own supervisor just went through a difficult divorce. And what helped her most was working harder, working longer hours.

ISOLATION: MOTIVES AND METHODS

She has no idea that my brain is a block of ice, that simply being awake and groomed and dressed and out and among people is taking more courage and grit and determination than I knew I'd ever be capable of. That if I let down my guard for a second, I'd be a puddle of goo, unable to breathe or be in this world.

The Shame of Grief

I felt that, because I wasn't feeling recovered after six months, or a year, or two, or three years, that I was failing at grief. I pulled back from honest connection because I was ashamed to have people know how awful I still felt, that I was lost, that I didn't know what I was doing or why I was even living anymore.

I turned down many invitations because I was afraid of what might happen. What if I drive the 40 minutes to get to my friend's birthday barbecue celebration, only to crumble when I get there and see happy couples together? I was terrified I would have a total meltdown, and that I would either be unable to drive home or would wind up causing a terrible accident as I tried to navigate the car while sobbing. So I made a lame excuse and stayed home.

The regular get-togethers with girlfriends over lunch became excruciating. We'd all known each other for most of our lives, since elementary school. I love them all. There's something very special about having friends who have seen you go through all of your different phases, from childhood through adolescence and adulthood. But even in that group, I felt isolated – because I didn't want to overwhelm them with how I felt, because I didn't want to risk crying in a restaurant over lunch, because I would feel guilty if I dominated every conversation with my grief.

So we'd get together, and we'd talk. And they'd tell stories about their children, and they'd complain about their husbands. And I would bite the inside of my cheek and dig my fingernails into the palms of my hands to keep from screaming. None of them have terrible relationships, their complaints were the garden variety annoyances that we've all had to some extent or other with our partners, me included. But to hear a complaint that a husband throws his laundry on the floor, when my husband wasn't alive to be able to throw his laundry on the floor … it made me furious, and hopeless, and I felt unseen. They didn't mean it; they were talking as we always did. I was the one who was hearing it differently. And instead of letting them know, I stayed silent. Isolated.

I thought that, if others knew how I was truly feeling, they would judge me for it. Why? I judged myself, that's why. I berated myself for being lazy, for being weak, for being indulgent. I compared my grief to that of so many other people who are suffering in this world, and I felt unworthy of so much distress. I have since learned that comparisons are never helpful, and that everybody grieves 100% of every loss. It makes no sense, nor is it helpful, to think my loss is less important or less tragic, and therefore less worth grieving. But I didn't know that yet.

I found myself unable to empathize with others' losses because I was so wrapped up in my own, and expending so much mental energy trying to hide my grief. About a year after John died, my sister lost one of her cats. She had taken two to the vet's office, and one had somehow escaped, run outside, and gotten into the surrounding woods. She was extremely upset about this, and normally I would have been completely sympathetic. I would have felt her pain and guilt, I would have been there for her to lean on. But I found myself completely unable to care, and that shamed me. I wanted to scream

ISOLATION: MOTIVES AND METHODS

at her, "Who cares about your cat? My husband is dead!" I'm pretty sure, and I hope I'm right, that she didn't realize at the time that was how I felt. I think I said all the right things, and I hope I was able to be some comfort to her.

Was I Failing at Grief?

I began to feel I wasn't grieving properly. Was it acceptable to acknowledge that he had bad habits and character flaws? Was it okay not to miss those aspects of him?

I also started to think about what my life would look like from now on. It was apparent that nothing could be the same, that "normal" had been obliterated. John wasn't here anymore. I didn't have my best friend or partner. Everything we'd ever thought of doing together was never going to be. Not only that, but this grief had transformed me. I wasn't the same person I was before John died. My perspective had changed in a profound way, so some of the aspects of my old life just didn't fit anymore.

I felt as if my life had been shattered into tiny pieces. I could pick them up and try to fit them back together, like a jigsaw puzzle, into what had been there before – but some of the pieces didn't belong anymore, and I realized that I could choose which ones to keep, which to discard, and what new pieces I wanted to acquire. I had an opportunity to create a beautiful new mosaic of my life. The old normal no longer existed, so it was up to me to build a new normal. In Chapter 7, you'll see that this concept of a mosaic reappeared once I was recovered from grief and ready to begin building my new life.

For now, I was frozen. It felt like it would be a betrayal of John if anything positive emerged for me because of his death. I knew I was at a crossroads and had to start walking a new path, but I just stayed in one place turning around in circles – not because I didn't know what I wanted, but because I felt obligated to stay in this place of sadness and grief and despair. It was my monument to my love for him. How could this new life, whatever my new normal was going to be, include creativity, hope, or love? Since he was no longer beside me to have these things, I felt it would be wrong for me to have them either.

Failing at grief,
I don't miss
angry outbursts
pessimism
cacophony.
Attempting to channel
mourning into creativity,
sadness into compassion,
I berate myself.
If I find a hopeful path
there is a positive to his death
All must destruct or he is betrayed.

I often heard people say, "He loved you so much. He wouldn't want you to be sad. He'd want you to move on with your life."

That infuriated me.

First of all, how do YOU know what he would want? And "he wouldn't want me to be sad?" I don't believe that. After all, if I'd been the one to die I would certainly want him to miss me and be sad I'd died! No, not stuck in pain for the rest of his life. But sad? Yes. And anyway, what does it matter what he would want? HE'S DEAD, he doesn't get a say. He left me here all alone, to figure all this out on my own. He forfeited his wishes by dying on me. After all, he obviously didn't love me enough to live.

Of course, a lot of this thinking was irrational, but it's exactly how I felt.

I would also go through phases of being terrified that I would forget him. I don't have the kind of detailed memory that remembers exact conversations or how things looked or even an accurate sequence of events. My memories tend to consist more of moments, of flashes, and mostly of feelings. I will remember how a book made me feel, but not what the names of the characters were or how the plot unfolded. I remember a happy childhood, with glimpses of games played and the people who made it fun, but not necessarily what we talked about or how the house was furnished or who did what, when.

And that scared me. The only thing I had left of John was my memories, and I was so afraid that they would fade. I struggled mightily to hang onto every bit of him that I could. I lived in fear that I would wake up one day and he'd only be a vague, distant collection of images.

That hasn't happened, although I do wish I had been able to retain a few more details. The fact is, I remember a lot of what we did and said – but I know I haven't held on to every bit of it. I'm never even quite sure I remember exactly what his voice sounded like, and that bothers me. I absolutely remember how he made me feel, and he made me feel happy and loved and secure and amused and exasperated and irritated and supported and trusted and respected. Those are memories that aren't just in my head, they're in my heart. And they lift me.

Sometimes, I felt cheated by how others remembered him. When John was out in the world, at work or with friends, he was such a positive presence. He made people laugh, he mentored them, he was always constructive. But John at home was different. He was everything he was out there, but there was another side that came out, too.

He was never mean, and he was never cruel. But he held a lot of anger, and it was at home that he was able to express it. The bottom of a yogurt container could break open, and he would kick a hole in a kitchen cabinet. A wiper blade could be hard to replace, and he would rant and rave. It was difficult for me, when we first married, to witness these things and not feed into the negativity. Early in our relationship, his anger would cause mine to rise, and we had some epic arguments. But I learned that, as he insisted, he was "just barking" and letting off steam. That home, with me, was a safe place for him to discharge those emotions. And I figured out how not to let it touch me, which in turn stopped the escalation.

But I was jealous. Jealous of the people who would come up to me and say, "John was always such a happy guy!" I'd think, "Why couldn't he have been happy with me?" But I realized, finally, that his behavior was a compliment. He trusted me to love all of him, and I did – even the parts I didn't like much.

That was also something that made me feel horribly alone in my grief, though. As I'd realized at the shiva, nobody else knew the man I knew. Even those closest to him – his brother, his best friend – knew more of him, but not all. I was the only person in the world grieving the man I knew, and that made me feel that nobody could understand me or help me.

Loss of Traditions

Losing my husband caused all sorts of secondary losses, as well. One of those was holiday traditions. Because John and I didn't have children, all of our holidays revolved around each other.

We loved sitting outside on Halloween after carving pumpkins. We celebrated each other's birthdays with multi-day extravaganzas that grew more elaborate each year. We became home base for my family on Thanksgiving, with John being the main chef. We celebrated both Christmas and Hanukkah, delighting in finding gifts for each other.

All of that changed when he died. And I found that often, I had no one to celebrate with now. Halloween lost its special glow and became a day to either be out of the house or hide with the lights out. Birthdays weren't special anymore. Thanksgiving became smaller and more contained.

Christmas was especially hard. I grew up in a Jewish household but always loved all of the non-religious aspects of the Christmas celebration. The lights, the tree, the music, the gifts, the wonderful sentiments of peace and joy to all the world. I was so happy that I married someone whose family celebrated that holiday, and I plunged myself into it. Whether visiting his family in Vermont, or hosting them at our house, I felt a lovely sense of belonging and celebration. I found concerts or ballets or plays for us to attend; organized trips to the local botanical gardens to see all of the decorated trees; and absolutely delighted in finding just the right gifts for each person.

John died on the Friday before Thanksgiving. So that year, all celebrations were off. I sent a box of gifts up to Vermont in December, thinking that his little sister shouldn't be cheated of her Christmas presents. And that was it. No more Christmases for me. The following year I hoped to spend the holiday with his family, but an invitation never came.

Now I try to enjoy the season and celebrate with my friends leading up to December 25, but on that day I am alone. It's not my holiday, it never was, so I'm at peace with that. But there's so much pressure, both internal and external, to experience the joy of the holiday season. And there's messaging everywhere about the importance of being with and treasuring time with family. All those TV movies about family being the only thing of importance! And my family is me. And my cat. My family of birth is scattered; we enjoy each other when we are together, and we love each other, and they have been wonderful to me. But it's a small family that doesn't get together for holidays. And every year, I feel the loss anew, and I feel alone.

Retreating from Life

I started spending a lot of time doing nothing. Days would go by, while I sat on my couch watching TV, playing video games on my phone, and eating junk food. I couldn't change the past, I couldn't bring John back and get back to the life I wanted, so irrationally and unconsciously, I tried to stop time by numbing my mind and body. I couldn't go back and had no desire to move forward. I'm grateful that I had the presence of mind not to drink any of the wine or whisky in the house. But I grew fatter and more sluggish as the weeks went by, dulling my body and brain from the pain of my grief.

I wanted to be a bear. I wanted to crawl into a hole and hibernate, to just sleep and sleep and sleep – and then, eventually, to awake to a world reborn, spring flowers and fresh air and new life. I actually

ISOLATION: MOTIVES AND METHODS

found myself wishing for a psychotic break. I wanted to be out of my mind, to go to a place where I didn't know reality.

Every fond memory, each good thing turned into pain.

Beautiful day out. 60 degrees, sunny. Took a walk around the block, then sat in John's bamboo garden for about 20 minutes. It will always be his garden – I can visit but it will never be mine. The breeze in the bamboo makes a calming, whooshing sound. He was so proud of this place. He transformed this scrubby patch of land at the side of the house, creating a peaceful spot where we could sit, could eat, could be.

It's so lovely out here, peaceful, tranquil. And I am overwhelmed by sadness and indignation. The bamboo is growing, the fronds are waving in the breeze, and John's not here to enjoy his handiwork. He created this lovely spot – his vision, his effort, his sweat. How can he not be here? And how can I move away from this house when so much of him is planted here? Part of me wants to run away, part of me wants to stay forever.

Another spring is coming. Another spring without John to tend the bamboo, go kayaking, hike. How can there be a spring without John Monsees to revel in it????

Sometimes, I'd have a few days when I started to feel better. When I could imagine a time when I could let go of the pain, when I would be happy to be alive again. And then another wave of grief would hit.

It's back. That feeling of futility – of not caring about anything because what does it matter? Yeah, I know that people love me, but it just doesn't seem to matter to me. So what? I'm unmoored, rudderless, drifting through the days, pretending that I'm living my life. But I don't want to make any more decisions, I don't want the hollow joys of everyday living, I don't want to act as though I'm still me. I'm not me. I'm not. I'm a shell. And I think about filling that shell up but I don't really have the energy to do it. Or the motivation, the desire.

The smallest thing brings me to tears again.

I want to go back to bed and sleep for a week. A month. A year. Two years, five years.

Everything hurts. The beauty of a sunny day. The drama of a windy day. The laughter of friends, the joy of music, the support of friendship. They just bring more hurt.

I want to be alone, on a rocky beach. I want the wind and the sand and the water to erode my nerve endings, to blast away all the feelings, to purify my soul.

I want John. I WANT JOHN.

This IS NOT my life!!!

I want to be a little girl, rocking in my mother's arms. I want to be comforted, but there is no comfort. No comfort.

Isolation doesn't always take the form of being alone. Sometimes I felt more isolated when I was with the people who love me most. A year and a half after John's death, my wonderful parents celebrated their 60th wedding anniversary. We all – my mom and dad, sister and brother-in-law, brother and new sister-in-law, and niece -- gathered to celebrate.

ISOLATION: MOTIVES AND METHODS

Mom and Dad's 60th wedding anniversary. Lovely, BUT.

I'm alone. I was cheated. Without warning. It all was ripped away. I'll never have 60 years – I never thought I would have, but I thought I'd have at least 30. Why do I have to be all by myself? It feels like I spent so many years, before I met John, searching for that connection, feeling lonely and unworthy and unanchored. And now that's back. But I've had the connection and will never have it again. Maybe I don't feel so unworthy, but lonely and unanchored? Oh yeah. Free floating, not in a good way. In a nauseating, terrifying free fall that never ends.

I spent all weekend playing the good daughter role, knowing that John would have been proud of me. But I was jealous of all of them. I wanted to scream, cry, run away.

I still want to scream, cry, run away. Fade away.

Grief, My Constant Companion

Grief became my best friend. It became my identity. It became my comfort. It was somehow comforting to hold on to the emptiness, the loneliness, the absence of John that was all I had left of him. It was my snuggie – a blanket I could wear all the time. It had sleeves, so I could get a few things done, but it weighed me down, kept me from moving out or forward, and separated me from the world. Retreating into the Grief protected me from having to deal with life.

So I continued to hibernate. Days melted away into TV watching, playing computer games, napping. I didn't feel better. My back ached, I was continuously fatigued, I had no interest in anything. And I was so very sad.

In a blink, I aged
Not ripened nor mellowed
From young to ancient
From spirit to fossil
From innocent to damaged
Wife to widow

This was written in my journal a little over four years after his death:

I miss him. I yearn for days past. I can't see a defined future. Anytime I begin to think about changes – moving, volunteering, exercising, training – I quickly fall back into nothingness. I get excited briefly, but it disappears. I don't feel capable. They say you're as old as you feel – I'm 80. I'm an old woman with my best years (such as they were) behind me.

I do believe we make our own destiny. That no matter what life deals us, we can find the positive, the light, the growth. But in practice, I find it's not so clear. My sadness is my shroud, my armor, my protection. If I don't have a good life, I have nothing to lose. Now that I know what it is to lose, I don't want to risk.

I can't even eloquently articulate what I mean, here.

I've emerged from a tunnel, but I'm sitting here at the entrance. If I venture too far afield, I might not be able to find my way back. The tunnel is darkness, isolation, fear. But it's what I know. It's all I can remember.

I'm stuck remembering what I've lost. Not remembering the love or the happiness, but the loss itself. And I fear that if I move on, if I finish processing this grief, then I won't feel close to him anymore. That I'll have some vague good memories that make me happy, but that I will have to have let go of him.

All through my adolescence and young adulthood, all I wanted was romantic love. To find someone who would accept me unconditionally, who would want to be with me above all others, who would be my partner in life. I finally found him, and he was so different from who I'd thought he'd be.

How could I possibly find another? Especially since I don't have as much to give. I was never a beauty but now I find this body disgusting. I'm not interesting, I'm not ambitious, I don't really want to do much. Who the hell would want to be with me? I don't want to be with me.

So the closest I'm ever going to be to being in love, to being in a committed relationship, is to immerse myself in what was. To be sad and missing John is the closest I can be to being in love. And I've always wanted to be in love, and I still do.

I came to believe that my grief was the only interesting thing about me. That without it, I was nothing. I also feared that abandoning my sorrow meant abandoning my love, and I was not willing to do that.

It is impossible for me to get back on track. The track I was on was built for two. I need to switch to a different track. But I don't want to. I'd rather stay just where I am, on this track that is impossible for me to navigate.

The Weight of His Absence

John had died, but I was refusing to leave his side. I knew I couldn't follow him, but I wasn't prepared to abandon our life together. I felt I needed to make my life a monument to my grief, that the only way to honor our love was to be miserable without him.

I'm sad all the time. Even when I'm out with friends, laughing, genuinely having a good time, there's an underlying awareness of the sadness. It's become my constant companion, this weight of the absence of you.

You'd think an absence would be a hole, an emptiness, that there'd be no heft to it. But that's not how it is. Your absence is ever-present and it weighs me down. It holds me in place, in time, in myself. It's not unwelcome – it's all I have left of you, so I cherish it. I embrace it as it surrounds me, fills me, holds me. It's the closest thing I have to your arms around me, to your voice in my ear, to your laughter, to your scent, to your essence.

It's like an afterimage, like the light in the eye after a flash photo – it's elusive, always moving. You can't focus on it; every time you try it floats just out of reach, back into the periphery. Sometimes it's different colors. Sometimes there's one light, sometimes a cluster. It's beautiful but it's not real, it's only a perception, an aftereffect of something that once was there.

I don't want to lose it. I don't want a day to go by when I don't think of you and feel the weight of your absence. I don't want you to become a collection of memories – I want to keep you with me. And if the only way to do that is to constantly feel the loss of you, to feel utterly alone, to feel weighted down by your absence, then it's a price I'm willing to pay. Anything to keep you as close as possible.

So. I will keep up appearances. I will "move on" by cleaning out the house, by getting out and being with friends, by pursuing interests and redecorating and writing. But there's a small, impenetrable box inside of me that holds the weight of your absence. And I will not give that up. I will not betray you by letting you go. You were taken, but I refuse to let go. I will remain loyal, and true. Even if I someday find another man for a companion, lover, husband ... I will protect the contents of that box in my soul that is you, that is us.

And I will welcome the daily tears. I'm not so good at remembering events. I'm not so good at remembering sights, smells, sounds. But I excel at remembering feelings. So I will hold on to our love, and how you made me feel ... smart, capable, sweet, optimistic, patient, silly, safe. Even if that means locking all of those things up in the box, with you.

I don't want you to be gone. But since you are, I want to miss you. Every day. Every. Day.

*they say I'll feel his presence,
he will always be with me.*

well.

*what I feel --
oppressive and always,
however I turn and wherever I go --
is his absolute and utter Absence.*

I did slowly come to understand, finally, that the grief was something to process, to go through, that I didn't want to stay stuck. But I knew it wouldn't be easy, and I knew I couldn't simply abandon the pain or turn off the feelings. If I denied the darkness it would only grow. I still had a long road ahead of me, and I still didn't have a map to follow.

I don't want to box it up, put the lid on, and shove it to the back of the closet. I want to hold it, love it, spend time with it, accept it, and let it slowly dissipate, let it sleep peacefully. It's like a mass of dark energy. If it gets shoved to the back of the closet it will fight to get out. If it's accepted and loved it will be at peace.

The pain is my baby. I've given birth to it, I must nurture it. It's not about feeding the pain, it's about recognizing it. Attention must be paid.

CHAPTER 5

Beginning to Recover (But Not Quite)

Pretenses

Progression out of grief isn't a straight line. There are advances and regressions, twists, spins, u-turns, and false starts. I found myself disintegrating: I was living my life, doing work, setting goals, performing tasks all the while feeling like the real me was still stuck in a dark place I could never fully climb out of. I began to come out of the shock of his death and realize that I would need to create a new life for myself, by myself. But I had no idea what that might look like, or how to go about it. And I desperately, desperately didn't want to have to do it. I was throwing a constant mental tantrum of NO NO NO NO NO NO, not wanting to accept the finality of his death. But it wouldn't do to let anybody know this, especially because I was convinced that no one would be able to help. So I pretended to get on with the business of living. It was as if I'd put on a robot shell, which looked and sounded and acted like me, while in reality I was sitting at the bottom of a well, hiding from the world.

Coming out of the shock was an important first step, but it had very unpleasant consequences. Coming out of shock meant feeling.

I've been avoiding thinking, feeling too deeply. I desperately want to go back to the first year, when I was in a fog. I want to keep that wall of jello around me, that protects me from the harshness of my reality. I feel vulnerable, naked, weak, fragile. Like walking in the truth will be like walking naked through brambles, it will rip off my skin. Gouging jagged rips, leaving blood and pain and infection in their wake. It burns, it stabs, it throbs.

Glimpses of Sunlight

From the moment John died and for years afterward, part of my mind engaged in magical thinking. It was convinced that, if I only did something just right or wished hard enough or loved well enough, the universe would reverse and I could get him back again.

As I slowly began to let go of that obsession, the difficulty of reality began to sink in.

I've almost stopped wishing him back to life – the active, energetic, if I just wish hard enough it will happen kind of wishing. I want him not to be dead, but I seldom still think that if only I had the secret, the key, the time machine, the path that I could bring him back. I'm not sure which is worse: the violent longing or the desperate resignation.

BEGINNING TO RECOVER (BUT NOT QUITE)

Then I felt as if I'd turned a corner. It happened both suddenly and gradually, while I was at a writing retreat.

Somehow, in the midst of the meditations and writing, something shifted, gelled. I know now, know deeply, that he is and will always be a part of me, and that A) I CAN remember him, remember our life together; and B) I don't have to hold on desperately to the grief and emptiness. Loosen my grasp and I see he's still there – HE is still there. I was confusing the sadness, the emptiness, his absence, with him. He is not the grief. I can let go of the grief without letting go of him.

This is HUGE. I feel, I don't know, whole again. Or almost. Like I can be whole again, which for a while I never thought would be possible.

Then, a week later, this emerged in my journal:

I realized that I've turned a corner, though that's not the right analogy. It's more that I've travelled through a series of connected tunnels. An underground labyrinth, catacombs. Gone deeper and deeper, then slowly on a shallow incline come back to the surface.

John's death dropped me deep underground. First I sat, huddled and scared, in a hole. Then began to feel my way blindly, a few halting steps at a time, with no direction. This way then that, not knowing or caring which route. Stopping along the way to sit in another hole with my head bowed, hands covering my face, knees to chest, no desire for direction or map.

Bit by bit, my forays became longer, I went a little further. But the tunnels didn't lead straight up – they went up, down, tilted, changed direction. What I couldn't see was that they did lead me in an overall upward direction. In the tunnel, I had no perspective. Couldn't tell where I was or might be headed. Blind, deaf, numb.

Without realizing it I've arrived near the end – the tunnels delivering me to a surface that is strange but not completely unfamiliar: similar to the old world but a new planet to explore. This is where I live now.

The first thing I knew was that nothing was normal. "Normal" had been obliterated. And when my world tilted on its axis I was plunged deep into the core of some new planet in an unknown dimension.

But even though I knew I had to figure out and build a new normal – knew that very early – before I could begin to create I had to peel away the dead rotting layers of the old normal. It had died but not disappeared. It was in my thoughts, habits, heart.

*Feeling my way, piece by piece. What to keep and revive, what to discard? What **must** be discarded regardless of attachment?*

There was no way to build a new normal until I had dealt with and processed and said goodbye to every part of the old.

And I couldn't see. Couldn't see the whole so had no perspective on the progress of my journey. Somehow, even without realizing it, I had trust that I was moving forward, that the work was worthwhile, that it would yield this new life, this new normal. Trust in myself, trust in the universe, trust in my friends, family, therapist.

The journey has not been easy or simple, or straightforward. The path through the tunnels twisted, some places narrow, some wide. Some narrow places were claustrophobic, some comforting like swaddling. Some wide places were airy and hopeful, some vast and endless-seeming deserts. Light varied – pitch black, deep purple, slate gray, hints of blue. Moments of bright light extinguished quickly. Not turned off, smothered by the darkness. Dark was animate. Not the absence of light but an elemental entity that was blanket, floor, air. It felt like I was moving in circles, in spirals. Headed up only to find myself down.

Without realizing it I was heading toward the light. Now that I am close to the surface, I feel the lessening of the pressure. If I'd risen too quickly I'd have the bends. It was absolutely necessary to wander, to stop, to go a few steps at a time. To simply rise up would have been to blast through layer upon layer of rock and darkness, leaving only rubble and stark blinding light. Bruises and lacerations and burnt retinas.

The slow, tortoise path has left its marks too. Sluggish brain, atrophied muscles, dilated pupils. But the old normal has been largely laid to rest. Time to begin building the new.

Although I had made significant progress, there was more work I needed to do. At this point I was still carrying all of the pain of my grief; I had only become strong enough to do so and still move forward with that burden.

What's Next?

Years of soul searching and therapy came together to remind me of what I knew all along.

The realization came when I was sitting on the couch with my cat, who was being very sweet and cuddly. This cat had been adopted shortly after John's death, and her name happened to be Hope. I was feeling very grateful for all the good things in my life, all the *love* – from Hope, friends, and family. And then I suddenly understood that I wasn't feeling guilty anymore for appreciating what was good – especially what was new – in my life.

*It's not that John's death resulted in good things coming into my life – it's just that there **is** good in the universe and if you allow it, it comes in to fill some of the gaps. The human spirit tends toward expansion.*

It's okay to enjoy life and beauty and love. Some of what's in my life now may not have appeared if John were still alive, but that doesn't make it tainted or lessen its value now. If John hadn't died, other – different and good things would be in my life. I've changed paths but that's no reason to devalue what I encounter on this one.

*And that **includes** what I encounter **internally**. Who knows how I would have grown as John's wife? That is an unknowable. The things I am developing now – nurturing myself, dealing with avoidance issues – I may or may not have confronted at this point in my life had John not died. Again, unknowable – although I probably wouldn't have sought therapy, so …*

*It still doesn't matter. **Even if** there's a direct cause and effect – John died, I'm in therapy, I'm dealing with my own issues – it still doesn't make it a bad thing to deal with those issues. It doesn't mean his death was positive. It just means my spirit is expanding in this direction now instead of another one (as John's wife).*

Remember, grief doesn't progress in a straight path. I would have these moments of clarity, these very strong realizations, then wind up under the blanket on the couch again for a few days. But it kept bubbling up.

I'm beginning to get a glimpse of a life beyond grief. Nothing concrete or detailed, just a whisper of a hint that I want to build a new life, a new normal. That someday I will be able to identify myself as something more than a widow.

Right now, that's my only identification. I am the wife whose husband has died. Everything I do, feel, think, is colored by that one fact.

Someday I think it will only be a portion of what makes me, me.

And I can take some time now to envision my future, what I want my life to be. Because we create our own futures, to a degree. If I have the courage to change the things I can, then I can become the person I want to be, the person I most want to live with every day.

I think that the Grief has become an old friend, a comfortable blanket. Retreating into the Grief protects me from having to deal with the world. And let's face it, I've never been confident about dealing with the world. Not just the world outside, but my own world. All the issues I've avoided dealing with for years. And while the Grief is real, it is also a convenient hiding place.

And my understanding deepened while my resolve grew.

I have spent the last years protecting others from my truth. It was too terrible to bear; how could I ask those I love to understand? I didn't want them to understand. I don't want anyone else to suffer what I suffer. But in protecting them I have hidden my true self. I give glimpses only. Glimpses into my soul, my suffering, my truth. Is that love? Can you truly love another and hide yourself away at the same time?

If I become stronger ... become different ... become more myself ... I fear that gives power to the grief, power to the darkness, power to death. But death does have power – I can neither diminish nor enhance that. Death has changed me. I inhabit a world wholly different from where

I was. And the only thing to do is adapt ... or die. If the consequence is that I become a version of myself I've always wanted to be, well, that's hard to take. It's still hard not to fight anything positive that would not be if John were not dead.

But I have been put on this path, in this forest where I can only find my way by forging ahead. I have to go places I've never been, do things I've never done, in order to survive. I have to learn to forage, to track, to be strong, to endure. Otherwise I starve or get eaten.

And the doubts still popped up. The fear of giving up the grief, of forgetting, of letting go of the pain was overwhelming. We tend to come back to what we know, to what's familiar, even if it isn't comfortable.

What happens once I tuck away the grief so that it is a part of my heart but not all-encompassing?

Do I lose John all over again?

John was my daily companion. He died, and grief took his place. The grief is a way of keeping him with me, keeping him close, keeping him alive. As long as I miss him, love him, mourn him every moment, he hasn't truly left me.

But once I actually start living the new normal, once I acknowledge the influences he had over me, the ways he will "always be with me" – then I will have to let go. The integrated grief is not a constant companion. And it feels a betrayal to let go of the pain, the emptiness. It will finally, truly kill him. If he is not missed, if his absence is not always felt, if I am not devastated, then he is truly and forever dead. And it must be. He is truly and forever dead, I cannot change that. But I feel like I'm holding him here with me, like the last bit of him hasn't disappeared if I am still sad, still not whole.

BEGINNING TO RECOVER (BUT NOT QUITE)

I did not yet understand that recovery from grief is not the same as forgetting. That I could learn to let go of the pain while retaining all of the memories. That was yet to come.

CHAPTER 6

This is Recovery

I Am More Than My Grief

What does it mean to "recover" from grief? It doesn't mean forgetting the person you've lost. It doesn't mean you won't miss them, or be sad that they're gone.

It does mean letting go of the debilitating emotional pain, and being able to smile again when thinking of them. It means being willing to fully connect with others again, and not shying away from relationships for fear of hurt.

After six years of journaling, reading, social networking, and therapy, I thought I was recovered. I had finally reached a point where I felt strong – strong enough to carry the burden of the pain of my grief. The pain was with me, always, and I assumed it always would be. The trick was finding a way to carry the burden but move forward in spite of it.

I thought I was better. In fact, I was better. I could sleep. I started to exercise, to eat more healthfully. I was able to enjoy moments with friends and family. But the pain of unresolved grief was ever present. Like an invasive vine, tendrils of pain wrapped around every memory and emotion, immobilizing my mind, spirit, and body and dragging me down into the depths of the earth.

But I thought I was better. I thought that life was as good as it was ever going to be.

Six years after John's death, I was ready to move forward. I knew I wanted a career change. Having survived this huge loss, I wanted to help others do the same. In fact, within the last few years it so happened that three different women I knew, all around my age, lost their husbands suddenly and unexpectedly. One was my brother-in-law's sister; one was my sister's best friend; and one was the wife of one of my husband's best friends. I found that I was able to reach out to them in those earliest, darkest days, and give them comfort and advise them. I found it very gratifying, and I decided that I would like to become a grief counselor, so that I could help more people. My old career, in the donor relations area of fundraising for colleges and universities, just didn't interest me as much anymore.

So, I began to look into graduate schools. I thought I might pursue a master's degree in psychology or clinical social work. What I found in my research made it clear why therapy hadn't helped me resolve my grief. Every single program I looked at offered only one or two classes in grief and bereavement! The only way I could see to specialize in grief would be to enroll in a program in pastoral counseling, and as someone who doesn't follow organized religion that wasn't appropriate for me.

But at least it suddenly made sense. Therapy had helped me in numerous ways – I confronted some childhood demons, I became more emotionally resilient, I was less anxious. But my grief remained a steady, heavy weight that I carried constantly.

Then I found something called The Grief Recovery Method®, and it changed everything.

Releasing the Burden

The Grief Recovery Institute® was founded in the mid 1980s by John W. James when he couldn't find anything to help him recover from the grief caused him by the death of his infant son. After a lot of research and experimentation, he developed a remarkable program that teaches people the tools and action steps needed to recover from grief. He and his partner, the late Russell Friedman, refined their Grief Recovery Method over more than forty years, and the Institute runs training programs all over the world, enabling Certified Grief Recovery Specialists® to teach the Method and help people who are suffering from all kinds of losses let go of their pain and move beyond the grief.

I attended a Grief Recovery Method certification course. I had no expectation that I would benefit from the program personally, because in my mind I was already recovered. After all, I was able to carry the weight of my pain. And the fact that I had enrolled in the training was my proof that I was ready to move on.

As part of the certification process, we participated in all of the action steps that are part of the Grief Recovery Method. We were meeting at a hotel, in late September. I'd made it a habit to take a short walk outdoors every time we took a break, to stretch my legs and get some fresh air. On the day we'd completed the final step of the Method, while on my customary walk I saw a dragonfly. If you've read Chapter 3, you may remember this memory I shared:

John and I used to vacation in Chincoteague, Virginia. We usually went in the middle of summer, but one year we were there in late September. On our last evening, close to sundown, we were making our last trip to the Assateague Wildlife Refuge. Suddenly we were surrounded by a swarm of dragonflies. Swooping, swirling, iridescent green, pink, and gold fairies filled the sky. We sat, transfixed, smiling in wonder at each other.

That was a beautiful memory, one of my favorite quiet moments spent together. But since he had died, it – like all of my memories – had become entangled with the pain that dragged me down, down, down.

When I spotted a dragonfly on that walk outside the hotel, I smiled, my mind instantly going back to that magical moment when my husband and I were relaxed, carefree, and sharing a rare experience. And I suddenly realized – I felt happy. Just happy! No pain, no dragging down, no instant of happiness swallowed by terrible sadness. My good memories had been restored to me!

I was flabbergasted. I never expected to benefit from the training in such a personal and profound way. It's not that my sadness is gone. I will always be sad that my husband is dead, and I miss him very much. But now I am able to truly enjoy and appreciate the good things – the memories of time spent together, the jokes he made, how he made me feel, the ways I've changed because he was in my life.

As a Certified Grief Recovery Specialist, I can help others as I have been helped. I am able to teach them how to restore their happy memories, move beyond loss, and thrive so that they can participate fully in all of their relationships again.

This chapter is about universal lessons I've learned about grief, from my training and the work I've done with other grievers.

You Can't Hide from Grief

Oh, you can try. You can distract yourself with healthy or unhealthy behaviors, you can stick your fingers in your ears, you can shut your eyes tight, you can socialize until you drop, you can hide yourself away from the world … but that's all temporary. You can't hide from grief, because it's a part of you.

There are over forty life experiences that can lead to feelings of loss, and grief. Some of them are obvious to most of us: Death. Divorce. Empty Nest. Retirement.

Some may be surprising, until you think about it: Graduations. Moving. New jobs.

And some losses are less tangible but no less real: Chronic illness. Change in financial status. Loss of trust.

All of us experience loss. With loss comes grief. And if we don't process the emotions of grief, it remains unresolved and complicates things the next time we experience loss.

Every individual is unique, so every individual's reaction to loss and grief is different. Grief is not a straight progression, from feeling bad to feeling better to feeling fine. Like most human experiences, it isn't linear – it's forward, back, back, forward, forward, back. Each person must go at their own pace, allowing themselves to not only feel their emotions, but to process them in a healthful way.

And because every individual is unique, and every loss is different, nobody can truthfully say, "I know how you feel." Even for people who have experienced a similar loss – widow to widow, parent to parent – all they know is how they felt, not how someone else is going to react.

Grief is Emotional

Grief is an emotional response to loss. It is not an intellectual response or a spiritual response. Despite that, most of what we say to grievers is either intellectual or spiritual in nature.

We say:

"Be grateful you had him in your life."
"At least she's not suffering anymore."
"There are plenty of fish in the sea."
"Rejoice, for she's in heaven."
"You will be reunited in eternity."
"He wouldn't want you to be sad."

I'm sure you can think of many other examples. Each of these has an implied "Don't feel bad ..." at the beginning of the statement ("Don't feel bad, be grateful you had him in your life."). Here's a secret – someone who is grieving feels bad! They deserve to feel bad. They will feel bad whether you tell them to or not. It's not a switch that can be turned off. Telling them not to feel bad won't change their emotions, but it may teach them to hide their true feelings.

Loss is cumulative, and unrecovered grief is cumulative as well. Here's an analogy I learned in my Grief Recovery Method training – we each come into this life carrying an empty backpack. Every time we experience a loss, a rock is put into the backpack. The rocks are different sizes, depending on the emotional significance of the loss. Some are small stones, some bigger, some are pebbles, and some are boulders. The rocks stay in the backpack unless proper steps are taken to recover from the grief of that loss. We walk around with this pack on our shoulders until we suffer the one loss that makes it just too heavy to carry.

Perhaps you've known someone who, upon experiencing what you'd characterize as a minor loss, goes into a tailspin of grief. It may be that the small stone, or even the pebble that symbolizes that loss, was just the last bit of weight their backpack could handle.

The Grief Recovery Method unpacks the load, and with each relationship that is healed the pack becomes lighter. If you are interested in learning more about the program, visit www.griefrecoverymethod.com or go to my website, www.ellenmonsees.com, for information.

Consequences of Unrecovered Grief

People may live for years with unrecovered grief, as I did, perhaps not even knowing it is possible to recover.

Although grief is emotional, the consequences of living with unrecovered grief may be emotional, intellectual, spiritual, and physical. It is common to experience any of these things in the short term following a loss, but if they persist and become long-term consequences they can have a devastating, negative effect on someone's quality of life.

Emotionally, you might experience pervasive feelings of overwhelming sadness, despair, pain, isolation, and disconnectedness. Intellectually, you could find you are having difficulty concentrating and are making poor decisions. Spiritually, many find they are angry at God, distrustful of their church and clergy, or have a loss of faith. And physically, unrecovered grief can manifest as lack of sleep, poor nutrition, illness, and accidents.

In order to find respite from the pervasive pain of grief, most people engage in what the Grief Recovery Institute® calls "short-term energy relieving behaviors", or STERBs. STERBs are ways of distracting oneself from the reality of grief, and they can be helpful in the short term. Some examples of widely used STERBs are drinking, drugs, gambling, workaholism, shopping, under- or over-eating, and increasing isolation. The problems occur when STERBs become substitutes for processing emotions, and move from short term to long term – or when the activity itself is harmful and dangerous.

Myths and False Beliefs

There is a lot of misinformation about productive ways to deal with grief. Unfortunately, most of what we've learned is how to distract from the emotions, not how to process them in a healthy manner. And all that does is leave those rocks in your backpack.

It just takes time. Give it time. Time heals all wounds.

Time does nothing except pass. If you have a deep cut on your arm, what matters? Time, or what you do within time? You can leave the cut alone, letting it get dirty and infected. Or you can clean and bandage it, allowing it to heal. The same amount of time will go by, but your actions determine whether the wound will heal, or fester.

Replace the loss. There are plenty of fish in the sea. You'll find someone else.

Sometimes, in an attempt to avoid loneliness, people will latch onto a new person after a loss. They will marry again within a year or less of their spouse dying. They will sign up on several online dating sites and play the field. Or they might replace the relationship they've lost with something different but all-consuming, like manic exercise or heavy drinking. These are behaviors we may have learned in childhood. Many parents react to a child's grief over the loss of a pet by saying, "Don't cry, we'll go get a new puppy on Saturday." Or perhaps you came home from school one day, told your parents you were sad or embarrassed because you were picked last for a team, and their response was to distract you by giving you a cookie and changing the subject. Many of us have learned to distract ourselves and replace what's lost before properly saying goodbye to what's gone before.

Grieve alone. Laugh, and the world laughs with you; cry, and you cry alone.

Be strong. Stiff upper lip.

These often go together: be strong, and if you can't be strong then grieve alone.

It can be inappropriate to allow yourself to be overcome with emotion in some circumstances. Unfortunately, that often expands to not allowing yourself to show emotion to anyone, in any circumstance. If only we were *always* permitted to show *some* appropriate emotion everywhere, we wouldn't be bottling it up. Suppressed emotions will almost always find some unexpected way to be expressed, often at inconvenient times and circumstances. They don't go away, they simmer, and repressing them robs you of honest, open connection with other people.

Keep busy. Distract yourself. Find a new project.

Most of us like to be seen as productive. Getting things done is a virtue. Many well-meaning people will advise grievers to find something to occupy their minds, thinking that they simply need to replace the sad thoughts with positive thoughts. It's not a bad thing to have goals, but when to-do lists and work are used to stop feeling, then the grief will wind up manifesting in some other way, some other time.

There are five stages of grief. Are you progressing through them?

This is one of the most pervasive myths about grief! When Dr. Elisabeth Kübler-Ross published her book, *On Death and Dying* (Scribner), in 1969, she identified five stages of grief. However, her work has been widely misinterpreted. Dr. Kübler-Ross had studied terminally ill patients, and she found that many of them experienced phases that she characterized as denial, anger, bargaining, depression, and acceptance. These stages were never meant to be applied to those left behind, the bereaved. They were only identified as common to those who were dying, not those who were mourning. (And even then, as she clarified later, not every single terminally ill patient went through every stage, and not every patient went through them in that particular order.) But the "stages of grief" have become very commonly known, and people may feel they're not grieving "correctly" if they don't go through every stage in the proper order!

Have I Recovered? How Do I Know?

You may have heard people say, "You never get over the death of _____." The blank in that sentence may be "child" or "spouse" or "parent", etc. I think that whatever truth is in that statement relies on what you mean by "get over."

Will I ever stop remembering my husband? No. (Absent a traumatic brain injury/dementia.) Will I ever stop wishing he hadn't died? No. Will I ever stop longing for his company? No.

But I am no longer stopped in my tracks, buried deep in pain, distracting myself from my world as it is, wishing for a different life. I am grateful and joyful and content for having had him in my life. My memories are completely restored to me – the happy memories are happy, the sad memories are sad, the angry memories are angry, the ridiculous memories are ridiculous. I see him, and us, as we truly lived, with all of the normal emotional highs and lows of a relationship.

Here is an example of how I know I have recovered: months ago, I was standing in line at the pharmacy waiting to pick up a prescription. The pharmacist asks name and birthday in order to identify the patient, and I heard the person in front of me say his birthday is March 16. It just so happens that my husband's birthday was also March 16. I noted it, but it didn't affect me emotionally. Before I had gone through the Grief Recovery Method, when I was strong but still carrying the burden of my pain, if I had heard that it would have sent me into a tailspin of despair. I would have had to work very hard to keep my composure, until I had completed my transaction and gotten to my car or house where I could break down and sob (because I had to Be Strong and Grieve Alone).

But more than that, I know I am recovered because I have a love for life again. I've recovered my capacity for joy. I am truly happy to have my memories of John. To me, recovery means the difference between visiting the land of grief versus living in it. Grief used to be my landscape. My body, my mind, my spirit were all buried in the rocky, barren tunnels of grief. Now, grief is a place I step into now and again. I feel sad, I cry, sometimes I sob and bawl. But it passes, and I can take my place back among the vibrant, living community of my world.

CHAPTER 7

Looking for a New Normal

Moving Through Grief

Grief isn't something that you get over. You can't simply wait for enough time to pass, or distract yourself by keeping busy, and expect the pain to go away. You have to process your emotions, move through the grief, and come out the other side.

Grief is exhausting! It's essential that you be kind to yourself when you are grieving, and allow yourself the emotional, mental, and spiritual space to sit with your loss and come to terms with the relationship that has ended or changed. If you are grieving, you may need to step back from some commitments temporarily in order to conserve the energy you need to process it.

Contrary to what you may fear, you will, in fact, stop crying. I know that there were times I fought terribly hard to hold back the tears, because I thought that this was going to be the time when I'd never be able to cease sobbing. Crying is not a weakness: to cry is to begin healing. Our tears have varying biochemical properties, depending on why they've been triggered. Emotional tears contain stress hormones, and crying is the body's way of flushing them out of its system.

It's also healthy to let yourself feel all of your emotions, even the ones you may judge as being "negative", like anger or regret. Trying to avoid those feelings doesn't make them go away, for they will reappear sooner or later. However, simply feeling the emotions may not be enough to allow you to recover from your grief. You're not only grieving the person you've lost (from death, or divorce, or other means), but you're also grieving all of the plans, hopes, and expectations you ever had for that relationship that now can't be fulfilled. You're not only missing what you had, you're also missing what you never will have. And, in some cases, you're missing what you should have had, or wanted to have, but never did – and now this loss has made it impossible to ever get it.

It's important to look at the entire relationship in a realistic way. Every long-term interaction contains emotional highs and lows. If we try to only remember the good ("don't speak ill of the dead"), we're robbing ourselves of the truth of the entire human experience. In the Grief Recovery Method, we teach our clients how to discover, and uncover, all of the emotional communications that need to be expressed in order to feel complete about the relationship. In so doing, they learn to remember and experience the full complexity of the relationship, and to let go of any pain due to regret or hurt.

Okay, I've Moved Through Grief. Now What?

It took me six years to fully process the grief of losing my husband. All of the work I had done, culminating in the Grief Recovery Method, finally allowed me to release all of the pain that had been weighing me down. Oh, what a relief! I felt lighter, more alive, ready to fully engage in life again.

But the life I had was no longer the life I wanted.

Grief decomposed me; it shattered me into a million little pieces. Now that I was strong enough, resilient enough, motivated enough to pick them up again, I realized that I had options. I could retain pieces. I could discard some. And I could acquire new ones. I was not, could not be, the person I was before. I had an opportunity to redefine myself that presented itself in a stark, obvious way.

The power had always been mine, but it was just so clear now. In the past it was difficult to change because of momentum, inertia, and the difficulty of tearing down in order to build up. But now my old self was already gone, and I had been presented with a clean slate.

My life wasn't a jigsaw puzzle. It wasn't a question of fitting each piece back together exactly and copying what was. No, my life was a mosaic! I could sift through, choosing some pieces, breaking others, picking up new ones, refitting them into a brand new pattern.

It was exciting. It was uplifting. It was hopeful. It was daunting, and terrifying. I began to ask some big questions. Who do I want to be? How do I become her? Is it too late for some things? If so, could they be modified to work now? I didn't know how to proceed. It's a big project, to put a whole life back together! Where should I start?

I felt confused. I didn't expect this. I thought I would grieve, then I would step back into my life. But my life without John, without our partnership, without our shared dreams and plans, seemed like a foreign land. Losing my husband had changed me, and my old life didn't quite fit anymore. I felt stranded and alone, yet ready to create something new. The obstacle now was in finding a way to envision and manifest the new life I would live.

In Chapter 1, I said that grief comes in waves. I realized now that I was like sea glass, being tossed and polished with each tumble. And I wound up more beautiful for having endured the process. I knew I could face whatever life had in store for me from now on; I just needed to find the right process to move ahead. The Grief Recovery Method released my pain. Now I went in search of a method to bring me joy.

Stuck in Thought Without Action

The biggest challenge I faced was putting action behind intention. I have great ideas, I plan well, I can visualize change. But follow through is not my strong suit. I have always lived more in my head and heart than in my actions. Frankly, my default has always been to sit on my butt. And since sitting on my butt is my weakness to begin with, the grief knocked me down and made my butt bigger and heavier – literally and figuratively. And while the grief was real, *it was also a convenient hiding place.*

Having been the youngest child in my family, I have perpetually felt like the little kid, the baby, the naïve one. I am the one who tries to be part of the group, who invents games to play, who is proud of her creativity, then is laughed at. I am the one who learned to keep her head down and follow directions, and to do what she is told, for that is what garners praise. Excel, but not too much. Don't stand out. Therapy, which I'd only sought because of the grief, helped me work through these issues to a great extent, but the behaviors and habits I'd used throughout my life to address them were going to be hard to change.

I had a little mental tantrum: I thought I was playing by the rules! I got married, I worked, I was nice. And the rug still got pulled out from under me.

How could I gain the courage to change my life, when I had never felt that I had real control in the first place?

Then I figured it out.

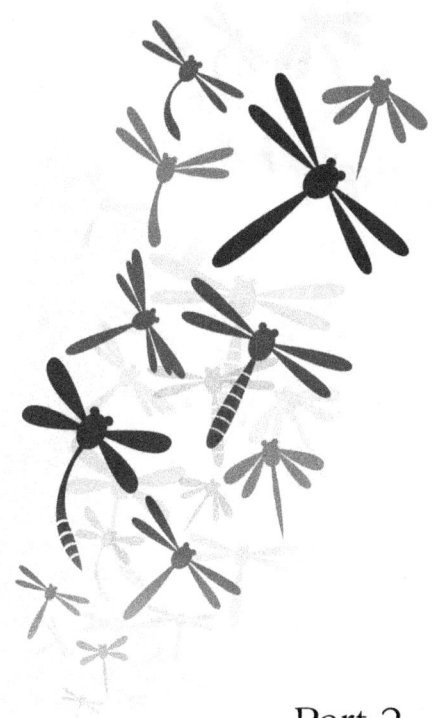

Part 2

Finding My Joyful Life

CHAPTER 8

Stranded in a New Land

I was lost. Once I had recovered from my grief, and my mind and spirit felt renewed, I was ready to step fully back into my life again. But I looked around and discovered that the life I had been living was gone. As if ravaged by a great natural disaster, like a tornado or earthquake, pieces were missing. Some parts remained, but there were piles of debris I would need to navigate in order to even get to the parts that remained. I felt like I'd been shipwrecked and stranded in a new land.

Not only had my life as it had existed been forever changed, so had I. Profound grief had changed me profoundly. Even if my old life had been there, waiting for me, I didn't feel like the woman who had lived in it.

I had never really lived intentionally; I had spent my entire life floating from place to place rather than swimming toward a particular destination. There was enough of a natural current that took me from school to college to jobs, and I had found enjoyment and fulfillment along the way. I wasn't consciously unhappy with how things had turned out. My life was fine, and I could have taken steps to pretty much step back into it as it was before widowhood.

I could force myself to try to reinhabit all my old patterns, but many of them would never really fit me again. And I realized that I could look at this as having been given an extraordinary chance: an opportunity to recreate my existence in a new way.

It didn't feel natural to just float back and insert myself once again into what had been, so instead I had to start swimming – which meant choosing a direction. As I understood that I needed to make some conscious decisions, I wondered if I dared seek more than I had before.

Jettisoning My Career

Six months after becoming a widow, I left my job and went to a new organization. As I've described earlier, I felt that I had no choice but to leave my previous place of employment when my beloved boss was replaced with a new director. I didn't feel safe with her, and given the generally heightened levels of anxiety I was feeling from grief already, I knew it wouldn't be good for my physical or mental health to stay in that environment.

I was lucky to find a position that, on paper, was the perfect fit for my experience and talents. But after struggling for a year and a half, I had to admit that I wasn't up to the task of building this new program. My grieving brain wasn't able to process information quickly enough, and my creativity was nonexistent due to emotional, mental, and physical fatigue.

In the extremely fortunate position of having the financial resources to support myself for a while without a job (hooray for savings and life insurance), I took the leap and decided to just stay home and allow myself to grieve. I took on a small amount of seasonal freelance work from my previous employer that I was able to do from home, but that was only a few hours a week, and not every week. That's when I did most of my reading, journaling, and social networking. It's also when I allowed myself to just stop for a while, and zone out in front of the TV and video screen. I continued with my therapy sessions and built up my emotional resilience and self-confidence. Eventually, I got myself to a point where I felt I could function again, albeit while carrying a constant burden of pain.

Addressing the Physical Ramifications of Grief

Speaking of pain, I was experiencing considerable physical discomfort as well as emotional distress. I had never been a naturally athletic or especially active person, and now years of grief-induced eating and sitting and sleeping had taken their toll. I had gained a great deal of weight, my muscles were weak from disuse, and the aches in my body made me feel at least twenty years older than my actual age.

Two years after I'd left full-time work, I found myself sitting on the couch watching TV (as usual), and I saw a commercial advertising electric scooters for disabled people. When I realized I was thinking I'd like to get one, because wouldn't it be nice not to have to walk around – something in me awoke. Here I was, middle-aged and fat, but generally healthy, and I was wishing my mobility away! That was the moment when I knew I had to start making some changes.

I had always been a naturally sedentary person. As a child, my preferred activities were all quiet and contained: reading, coloring, watching television, playing board games. A game of catch with a couple of friends and some swimming in the summers were my most athletic moments.

This pattern continued into adulthood. I always had jobs that kept me sitting at a desk. I went to concerts and plays. I sang, I read, I learned to make pottery and jewelry. None of these things had me moving around much. And in my grief, I increased my couch time from "a lot" to "almost all the time."

At various times in my life I had joined gyms with the intention of getting fit, but seldom took advantage of those memberships. I'd go to a couple of classes, or walk on the treadmills, for a few weeks or months. Then I'd fall back into my old sedentary patterns.

I knew I was at a tipping point with my health, and I knew that my old habit of joining a gym but not using it wasn't going to help me. I was perceptive enough to understand that this time, something had to be different and I needed to ask for help – I couldn't do it on my own.

I needed to be held accountable for my actions. Never having been naturally athletic, I required a coach who could teach me what to do and how to do it.

I was scared. My body was failing me. I was in pain. I wasn't sleeping well. It was becoming difficult to just stand up from a sitting position. I felt like an awkward, lumbering, fat old lady, and I was ashamed. My current condition was like reliving being picked last in the schoolyard for team games every day, but this time *I* was the one who was not choosing me.

I don't know where I got the courage or gumption to actually do it, but I remember looking up the phone number of the local gym where I'd had a membership before (when John was alive, and we both belonged), and making the call. I was physically trembling, my heart was racing and my stomach was doing flip-flops. But I managed to call and ask about personal training.

Somehow I forced myself to have an honest conversation with the manager of the personal training department. I described myself: middle-aged, obese, completely out of shape, never comfortable with my body. He asked me my goals, and I told him I wanted to lose fat, gain muscle, and improve flexibility and balance. I remembered to let him know that I would need a trainer who coached in a positive way. I respond well to encouragement and praise, not to criticism. A "drill sergeant" type of coach would only scare me away.

And I was so lucky. He suggested I make an appointment with Vicki.

Vicki turned out not only to be the perfect coach for me, she also has become one of my dearest friends. She is skilled at knowing how much she can push me; she has introduced me to activities, like boxing, that I would never have thought I could do or enjoy; and she has done it with love and joy and positivity that speak to me and motivate me. I have absolute trust in her, so I can work through my fears knowing she literally has my back. I have discovered a level of grit and determination that I'd thought were foreign to my being. I am stronger, I am more flexible, and I am more confident physically than I've ever been before. Despite some bodily challenges that have come with aging, I relish pushing my muscles and endurance to the limit during our sessions. And because I love and respect Vicki, I want to do better so that she will be proud of me and so that she will get the satisfaction of a job well done. We work hard, but we also laugh a lot and occasionally burst into song. As I write this, we are approaching our fourth anniversary of working together, which is – by far! – the longest time I have continued any sort of exercise program.

Making this one change – beginning and sticking with an exercise program – helped lay the foundation that allowed me to begin making other changes in my life. Aside from the health benefits it afforded me, like increased mental and physical energy and more restful sleep, it showed me that I was capable of intentional transformation. But it wasn't a magic cure, and my metamorphosis didn't happen all at once.

Creating and Picking Up New Pieces

John's death and my grief destroyed the jigsaw puzzle that had been my life. Until I found the Grief Recovery Method®, I had a very hard time viewing myself as anyone other than the one who mourns, the widow. But even before I started thinking about it consciously, I actually had begun picking out new things to include in my new existence, which has taken on a form that is more mosaic than perfectly fitted jigsaw pieces. It's not as neat or symmetrical or self-contained, but it is beautiful and expressive.

Making that phone call to find a personal trainer was the beginning of the forging of my new foundation. Another part grew from the problem I was having in my kitchen.

After my husband died, one of the things I stopped doing on a daily basis was washing the dishes. It wasn't even a difficult task (I own a dishwasher) but at the time, every single chore felt onerous, and I just couldn't deal with it. All I wanted to do was sit. Sit on the couch, watch television, and try not to feel or think about what my life was now that I'd lost him.

So the dishes would pile up in the sink. And every morning when I came downstairs and entered the kitchen, I would see the dirty dishes and feel weighed down even more.

Then, one day, I began to think about my Next Day Self. I am a fan of science fiction and especially enjoy stories about time travel. In most of those books, there is a "rule" that someone from the future must never interact with their younger self, because it would cause a paradox for two versions of the same person to exist in the exact same time and place, and that would make something very bad (like the total implosion of the universe) happen. But there was a novel I enjoyed very much, *The Time Traveler's Wife* by Audrey Niffeneger, that turned that trope on its head. In this book, the character who travels through time visits himself at various points in his life.

That concept had stuck with me, and now as I looked at the dishes in the sink, felt the weight of them, and wanted to just turn around and walk away, I thought about what I could do for a future version of myself. Instead of thinking, as I'd been doing, that "I'll be happy tomorrow if I do the dishes today" -- which wasn't enough to inspire me to action -- that day I thought, "*She'll* be happy tomorrow if I do the dishes today." Like many people, I often find I'm more willing to inconvenience myself for the sake of another person than to do something to benefit myself. I decided to care enough about my future self to make a small sacrifice in the present to support her. And I did the dishes.

The next morning, I came downstairs and walked into the kitchen, having forgotten completely that I'd washed the dishes. And I saw the clean sink and counter, and a smile lit up my face. I felt lighter. And I said, out loud, "Thank you, Last Night Ellen, for doing the dishes! I really appreciate it!" And then Last Night Ellen spoke up, out loud, and said, "You're welcome, This Morning Ellen! I'm so glad it made you feel better." It felt like, as in *The Time Traveler's Wife*, both Ellens were there, together.

It was an amazingly effective technique. My past self received love and acknowledgment for what she had done, which was validating and felt great. From that point on, I did the dishes almost every day. And every morning, I had the conversation among my selves. After a few weeks, it ceased to be spoken aloud and didn't even have words, just an internal nod of acknowledgment.

This is important: There were some days that I just could not muster the small amount of energy it would take to do the dishes. If I'd simply let them go, I'd likely have come down in the morning and thought ill of my past self for not helping out. So instead, if I really couldn't make myself wash the dishes, I would initiate another conversation, saying to my future self, "I'm sorry, I just can't do the dishes tonight." And then, in the morning, I would say to my past self, "That's okay, Last Night Ellen. I remember how we felt; I can take care of them today." Without realizing it, I had introduced an element of apology and forgiveness that turned out to be the key to keeping the loving relationship among my selves and formed the basis of much of the construction of my future life mosaic.

Choosing to Live Intentionally

It was a year and a half after I had begun working out, and two years after I had started doing the dishes again, that I went through the process of the Grief Recovery Method. Six years after becoming a widow, I was finally freed from the heavy burden of pain I had been carrying and felt ready to begin my new life.

It was time to begin putting that mosaic together, but how? Could I really begin to live consciously and intentionally? Who did I want to be, and how could I get to be her?

I thought back on the few things I'd managed to accomplish despite the pain of my grief, like going to the gym and doing the dishes. And then I remembered a powerful vision I'd had in a meditation:

I begin wrapped in silk the color of early sunrise.

I find myself in a room with tall gray walls, no windows. I am gazing at myself in a mirror when I turn around to see all of my selves – past and future. So many possible future selves! Some old and wrinkled, some crouched in pain, some straight and gentle. All the selves of all the days to come. Sad, lonely, sanguine, laughing, smiling, loving – all loving this present self. And the children, the girls, the young women, all of the past selves that have created this one. Oh, the innocent, the self-conscious, the brave, the broken.

Now I am shooting through space. I see all of the stars in the blackness. I know I am part of them, that starlight fuels me. Then I shift and am swimming. On a dolphin's back I glide through silver water that streams off my body, making me feel smooth and sure.

Coming to rest, I am sitting in the sand. The sun overhead is warm and the ocean breeze is cool. I smell salt and seaweed and hear the steady rhythm of the waves as the water undulates in its ancient dance. I feel the pull of the tide in this place where life begins. It cleanses me, empties me, preparing me for any future I choose.

I am engulfed in love and exactly where I am supposed to be. There is no hurry, no need to decide where I am going. There is nothing but life and time and love and the source of all things. For now, I sit and wait, thanking each past self for her gifts, forgiving and embracing her one by one.

The future selves smile and nod. They will be there in all good time. Right now this is my moment, me alone. Made of, but free from, the past. Living in the stillness before the yet to come.

There was a time the emptiness felt empty, terrifyingly endless and lonely. Now the emptiness is full – replete with possibility.

And I realized that bringing my past, present, and future selves together could guide me toward a more centered, joyful, authentic, and purposeful life.

I am made up of many selves. I am the person I am now, in this moment: the Present Self that was created from all of the experiences I've had and choices I have made throughout my life. I am, also, all of the Past Selves I have ever been. Every phase I've gone through, every decision I've made, every emotion I've experienced, every lesson I've learned have not only molded me into the Present Self I am today, but are also still with me.

And I am all of the Future Selves I may ever be. Just as every Past Self has played its role in manifesting the person I am right now, my Present Self is one of the Past Selves for my Future Selves. Every choice that I make right now, every experience I have right now, how I deal with every emotion right now will create my Future Self. There are an infinite number of Future Selves I may become. And, while I can't control everything that happens in my life, I can take responsibility for my reactions and choices, allowing me to consciously direct which Future Selves come into being.

The tough questions now were:

Who do I want my Future Self to be?

and

How do I change my old ways of thinking and doing in order to live intentionally?

CHAPTER 9

The PPF Method™

The answers to the questions asked at the end of the previous chapter led to my creation of The PPF Method. "PPF" is shorthand for "Past, Present, Future."

My Past Selves

As I thought about this concept of Past/Present/Future Selves and using them to live intentionally, I remembered something that had come to me on vacation, just about six months after my husband had died.

I had gone on a trip with my best friend to a beautiful spa resort in the Pocono Mountains of Pennsylvania. This was a place that offered classes in art, yoga, meditation, healthful eating, and spiritual living as well as spa services like massage and facials, and had a large swimming pool and hot tub in addition to lush but manicured grounds.

As we settled into our week of relaxation, I was finding myself confused and uneasy. There were so many choices of things to do that I was overwhelmed. I felt that I "should" go to yoga and meditate, but that what I really wanted to do was just relax and read. I worried that I was avoiding activities just because I might not be comfortable doing them, even if once I'd participated I might gain great benefits and really love them. It really sent me into a spin of "maybe I should do this, but what if I do that, but I should take advantage of being here to try this other thing …" and the stress was building up. Why couldn't I simply settle in and enjoy my time away?

And I realized that, over the course of a sixteen-year marriage and wonderfully interdependent relationship, I had made some compromises, as we all do. In order to live harmoniously I put some things on the back burner while emphasizing others more – as did my husband. We were strong individuals, but we also functioned as a unit.

Without the other half of my unit, it was necessary to reassert my Self, but I'd lost sight of who that was without him. So something as simple as enjoying a week at a luxurious spa had become stressful and disorienting!

I decided I needed to make a concerted effort to remember who I was: who I had been, and who I had become. In a beautiful, peaceful, secluded spot, I sat down with my journal and a pen and made a list. I asked, "What do I love? What makes me happy? What brings me tranquility, serenity, peace, joy?" and determined to answer those questions honestly and without judgment.

As the list started to take shape, it grew. I remembered joy-filled events. I remembered sensory experiences: sights, sounds, smells, and tastes that just stopped me in my tracks, because they were so enjoyable

I needed to savor them. I remembered activities that so captivated and engrossed me that I lost track of the passage of time and the outside world. (It was necessary to distinguish between activities that made me lose track of time because they put me in flow with my centered self and recharged my mental or spiritual or physical energy, and the ones that I used to distract myself from emotions or discomfort – those activities, like lying on the couch watching TV all day, that can also make the passage of time disappear but were a drain on my energy. I tried to think of it this way: if I were an electronic device, would engaging in this activity be like plugging in to recharge my battery, or would it drain my power, making me increasingly slower and sluggish?) My mind skipped around, brainstorming and recalling all these things.

And when I was done, and I looked back at the list, I felt at peace. I felt more centered. I stopped judging myself for what I was or wasn't doing with my week of vacation and was able to settle down and enjoy myself.

Now I was thinking about that question of who I wanted my Future Self to be, and I remembered this list I had made while I was on vacation. I found the journal it was written in and started to look for patterns. Here is the list as I made it, in its random order:

The smells & sounds of the woods
Water
Lavender
Massage
Tropical colors & flowers
Cats

Dogs
Pottery, jewelry making
Romantic comedies
Musicals
Learning languages
Playing board games, card games
Butterflies
The full leaf of May
A cozy fireplace
The first day of school
Planning a trip
Editing, proofreading
Enjoying a meal that I have cooked
New makeup
Floating in a sensory deprivation tank
Playing jacks
Finding recipes
Researching colleges
Singing
Hanging clothes on the line
Polishing furniture
Dancing to the oldies
Reading
Candy
Sitcoms
Weeping willows
Lilacs
Honeysuckle

THE PPF METHOD™

Fireflies
Ladybugs
Badminton
Sleeping
Gadgets
Caviar
Champagne
Belgian chocolate
Naps on rainy days
Lions
Science fiction
Sunlight/long days
School supplies
New clothes
Halloween
Fall foliage
Scent of burning leaves
Ginger
Hot cider
Thanksgiving
Buying presents
A strong, warm shower
Pedicures, reflexology
Scent of new-mown grass
Smell, sound, and sight of ocean waves
Waterfalls
Rainbows
Colors

I reviewed the list, which I had begun to think of as my List of Joys. I realized that these were things that made me really, truly happy. They made me feel whole, they made me feel … well, they made me feel like me.

I know that I am an introvert, so it was not surprising to see that many of my Joys are quiet things, enjoyed in solitude. I am sociable, and I care about people, and I can be exuberant and happy in a group. But I also need to set aside personal time away from family and friends, because the right amount of time alone is what recharges my energy and allows me to be a better friend and companion. It was good to be reminded by my List that the small quiet things rejuvenate me and give me a profound feeling of peace.

And now I realized that my List of Joys was a great jumping-off point for thinking about what I wanted my life to include, and how I wanted my future to unfold. It gave me clues about how I could transform some of my daily living habits into healthier, nurturing ones, in a way that is very particular to me and how I respond to things.

I realized that all of the things on my List are still part of who I am, and many of them are things I could find ways to reincorporate into my life, or to appreciate in a more mindful way when they appear. My Past Selves had these experiences, and since all of my Past Selves had a role in creating my Present Self, my Present Self can recall all of these things at will. It's not just a question of remembering that I liked to swim, and then finding a pool I can use now. It's also the ability to call to mind – and body – exactly how each of the things on my List feels. Every joy of the past can still be a part of who I am today.

For example, if I close my eyes, and breathe deeply, and cast my mind back to my childhood, I can be a ten-year-old girl, on a summer afternoon, in the pool at the swim club. I am completely carefree, the weather is warm, the sun is bright, there are a few passing clouds. I see adults sitting at tables playing cards, I smell chlorine and cocoa butter and the mouth-watering aroma of hamburgers and French fries wafting down the hill from the snack bar. I hear the splash of the water and indistinct conversations, laughter of children and birds chirping. I have nowhere else to be, I'm responsible for no one. Going deeper into this daydream, I can feel the cool liquid as my arms and legs slice through the water. I feel my long hair streaming behind me, and I am a mermaid heading home to my magical kingdom.

At the same time, my past does not have to limit me. I have been formed by all of my past experiences, but they don't have to define who I am right now or who I will become. I know that my Past Selves can help me understand why and how I may react to certain things and people, and that they contain many lessons about what I do and do not want in my life. My Past Selves experienced sadness as well as joy, of course, and a myriad of other emotions as well. All of them provide lessons and guidance.

Every moment involves a choice. Every moment gives me an opportunity to decide whether to allow something in my life, or how to respond to a situation. Every single moment contains a choice: stay or walk away, be kind or be mean, breathe or tense, relax or resist, fight or flee, love or hate, connect or isolate. My Past Selves give me valuable information to help me make the choices.

My Present Self

Once I'd remembered what brings me joy, I saw that I had a powerful tool for making every day a more fulfilling one for my Present Self.

I started by noticing all of the sensory experiences that made it onto my List of Joy, like honeysuckle, fall foliage, ginger, and the scent of new-mown grass. Then I just tried to be aware. Any time I am presented with one of those sensory experiences, I stop – even if it's just for a moment, before I open the car door or step into the meeting or go down the stairs or begin to put the groceries away, and enJOY it. I focus on being fully present and acknowledging that this is a thing that makes me feel happy or peaceful or giddy. I breathe it in.

I have found that just paying attention can bring many of my joys back into focus on a daily basis. Some of them simply appear to me, like a particular shade of blue, and some of them are things I can consciously will into my day, like buying my favorite flowers and then remembering to notice and appreciate them.

Even when I'm having a difficult day, a moment or two of a sensory joy, fully felt, can put a whole different spin on how I'm feeling.

Focusing so much on joy, and being happy, made me wonder: am I being selfish? What's the difference between selfishness and self-care? Where do I draw the line?

When I think about leading a happy life, it's not all hedonism, or pure enjoyment. It is feeling as if I am centered to my core, connected to the Source of all things, and a sense that I am anchored and doing what is right, for me, at this time.

I believe that feeling fulfilled is the best path to being not only a happy individual, but a caring and nurturing companion, neighbor, friend, partner, parent, or child. When we allow our actions and intentions and attention to align with those things that we respond to naturally, we're no longer using a lot of energy trying to be something we're not – energy that could be redirected and used to serve others in some way. We've all had the experience of having a friend or colleague who is perpetually down in the dumps, or angry, or difficult. Those people aren't easy to be around, because they drain your energy. I don't want to be one of them; I want to be someone who inspires and brings peace or fun or love or advancement because I give off that energy just by allowing myself to be filled with joy.

We are all better for others when we are better for ourselves.

My Future Selves

I had brought the Past into the Present, beginning to infuse my current Self with all of the things that had given me joy throughout my life. I could relive those joys whenever I liked, and I'd begun to pay attention and take notice of all the joyful moments.

So now it was time to figure out how to bring all of this into the Future.

In each moment, a new Future Self is born. Everything I experience, everything I think and feel, and every decision I make determines which of an infinite possibility of Future Selves will come into being.

It's a freeing and exciting and daunting concept.

I know that I am the main character – the protagonist, or sometimes, antagonist – in my life story. I react and think and feel according to the attributes of that character. But I am also the author of my life story, and I can change things about my central figure any time I want to. The way I think about myself will influence the way I act. If I repeat to myself often enough that I am insecure, I won't feel safe. If I tell myself I'm not creative, I won't try to make something new. If I tell myself I am loving and strong and kind, I will manifest those characteristics.

These are things I do anyway, so why not do them mindfully and with purpose? I began to have some fun imagining possible futures for myself. I thought about who I wanted to be five years from now; one year from now; a week from now. I played with the possibilities … ten years from now I could be this person, or that person. I tried on different Selves to see how it would feel to be them.

I used my journaling time to flesh out these different personas, changing them each day, letting my imagination soar. At the same time, I was careful to keep my visions within the realm of possibility. I knew I couldn't switch from being an introvert who prefers being with one or two people or a small group of friends, to being an extrovert who thrives on going to big parties every night. But I could imagine versions of myself who had changed incrementally, over time. I knew I couldn't lose fifty pounds in a month … but I could in a year, or two, if I took the steps to do so.

It occurred to me that most of us tend to live up, or down, to expectations. I wanted my own expectations to be joyful, and kind, and centered.

I was loving this concept of learning from my Past Selves to inform my Present Self to intentionally create my Future Selves. But I struggled with putting it into practice.

CHAPTER 10

Bringing the Selves Together

Using The PPF Method is a lot like driving a car. My Past Selves gained the driving skills, remember where I've been, and have learned to handle different situations, such as what to do if I find myself in a skid. My Present Self is keeping her eyes on the road, in the present moment, both enjoying the scenery and avoiding hazards. And I am heading toward my destination – my Future Self. I can choose various paths to get to the same place, going direct on the highways or taking the back roads.

Now I picture myself not as one person, but as collective. I am a hive of Ellens, a community of Past, Present, and Future Selves. They can interact with each other. Every moment has become an opportunity to honor my Past Selves, thank them for their lessons, and heal them with my love. Every moment is also an opportunity to create, in awareness, my Future Selves.

Sometimes I find it's helpful to think about all of my Selves as working for an organization. I am the company, and my Present Self is the Chief Executive Officer.

It has been my experience that the companies with contented, motivated, productive employees are those that respect them as individual human beings rather than soulless human resources. A manager who is respectful, who sees employees as people working with her instead of for her, who sees herself as part of the team rather than separate from it – that boss cultivates an environment where each person is freely giving their best. They are happy to put in extra effort, not only because they will be recognized for it, but also because they like and respect the team leader and desire to make her happy as a person, not just a manager.

Similarly, if my Present Self treats my Past and Future Selves with respect, we will live in harmony. Honoring my Past Selves makes me whole; respecting my Future Selves causes me to make better decisions.

Being My Own Best Friend

Like many people, I can be hard on myself. I have scolded myself for not being good enough, or productive enough, or generous enough … you name it. While I was working with one of the therapists I'd gone to for grief counseling, we began to address this. I remember that she asked me whose voice it was that I heard when I imagined someone telling me I "should" or "shouldn't" do something. She explained that, often, that voice comes from memories of a strict parent or other authority figure.

I thought about it and thought about it, but I couldn't answer her question. I had no idea whose voice was in my head. It was neither of my parents, it wasn't a teacher, it wasn't another relative.

But now I know. It is my own voice, but in the form of a Past Self. Sometimes a Past Self holds regret over something she did or didn't do, and she can't let it go, so that "should have" loop gets repeated over and over in my brain. And I've discovered the secret to quieting that voice: being my own best friend.

I'm fairly self-aware. I knew, when I sought out a personal trainer to help me get my body healthier, that I needed someone who would encourage me with positivity. I knew that a drill sergeant type of trainer would have the opposite effect on me than I wanted – that I would mentally cower, be afraid to try (and possibly fail), and that I would quickly give up.

Well, that voice in my head full of "shoulds" and "shouldn'ts" was like a drill sergeant to me. I cowered from her. I stuck my fingers in my ears, sang lalalala to drown her out, distracted myself with unproductive behaviors like television watching … but she persisted.

She persisted, while I resisted. I didn't want to hear it. And she needed to be heard.

Then, one day, as I thought about my Past, Present, and Future Selves, I understood. And I let her – the Past Self who wanted desperately to be heard – speak. Just as when my two selves communicated about the dishes, I now sat down with her in my imagination. I let her speak, and I listened as if she were my best friend or my beloved sister. I treated her with respect, love, and care. I let her have her say. And whether it was a Past Self of years ago or a Past Self from five minutes before, it turned out that being heard was mostly what she needed.

Negotiating Among My Selves

As I was emerging from my years of grief, I found I was having difficulty in determining when it was the right time to be easy on myself and give myself a break, or when it was the right time to push myself to do something that made me uncomfortable but would be good for me in the long run. There were usually two voices in my head, which I'd labeled Lazy Ellen and Judgmental Ellen, arguing about what to do and berating me for whatever choice I'd make.

The PPF Method showed me that those were the wrong names for the voices. They weren't Lazy and Judgmental! They were actually Present Ellen and Future Ellens. Present Ellen wants to take it easy, be comfortable, have fun, and relax. Future Ellens want Present Ellen to take action that will make their lives better.

I saw that it didn't need to be a conflict, that one voice didn't have to win while another lost, and I certainly didn't need to berate myself for making choices. It was, rather, a question of negotiating with the voices, and creating a win-win situation. Present Ellen could do something for the benefit of a Future Ellen, and then she could relax and do something fun. Future Ellen would then thank that Ellen for what she'd done, and then, when she became Present Ellen, she could pay it forward by doing something for the benefit of another Future Ellen.

This was the breakthrough that I'd needed, and it was the beginning of a whole new way of living with joy and purpose.

Seeking Balance

I am a person who loves immediate gratification. I'd rather eat the cake now than refrain because it has too many calories. I'd rather buy the cute earrings than save the money. I'd rather sit cozily on my couch than get out of my comfort zone and participate in an activity that may or may not turn out to be something great.

In thinking about my desire for immediate gratification, and how many times I indulged it, I realized that what I was doing was satisfying my Present Self without consideration of what that would mean for my Future Selves. My Present Self is very strong-willed, and she wants what she wants, and she wants it now – of course, she wants it in the Present, while she is here!

Once I realized that all of my potential Future Selves were already a part of me, and how much I love them and want to nurture them, I began to break some old habits that were solely serving my Present Self. It wasn't easy, didn't happen all at once, and it's an ongoing process, but I learned how to negotiate among all of my Selves to come to decisions that were best for all. It's a technique that works for both short-term and long-term situations.

This technique also works for people who are opposite from me, and more often deny their Present Self in order to set things up for their Future Selves. Because if you constantly do that, then you're always living for a Future that your Present Self will never see, and you're living without joy in the everyday. It's so important to balance living for the Present with living for the Future! The Present is all we are guaranteed. But if, as I was often doing, we never make choices with an eye to the Future, then we set ourselves up for becoming less than we can be or desire to be. I had to learn to consider both Present and Future Selves, while keeping in mind lessons from Past Selves. And the good news is, they can all talk to each other and figure it out together.

The Four Elements of a Healthy Relationship

The Grief Recovery Method taught me that unrecovered grief is due to emotional communications that we've never said, or feel were never heard, or simply need to be said again. Discovering what these communications are for a specific loss, and expressing them in a particular way, are the major final steps in the process that helped me, and has helped countless others, release the pain of grief. The communications fall into three categories, encompassing apologies, forgiveness, and other significant emotional statements.

I now understand that expressing these emotional communications can also heal and strengthen my own relationship with all of my Selves. By apologizing, forgiving, and being emotionally open within my Selves, I am able to release regrets and "shoulds" and stop holding myself back. To the apologies, forgiveness, and significant emotional statements, I will also add gratitude. It is vitally important to thank my Past Selves when they serve my Future Selves, as it completes the circle of caring.

The Power of Forgiveness

Much of what I've learned about forgiveness and its importance in healing relationships comes from The Grief Recovery Method.

Some people are repelled by the thought of forgiveness, because they think it means the same thing as absolution, or excuse, or carte blanche, or it's a "get out of jail free" card. It is none of those things. Forgiving someone, whether it's another person or one of your own Selves, is an act of giving up resentment over a perceived wrong.

It's a decision to not hold on to negative emotion, to let go of blame, to acknowledge the wrong but discard the hurt. It is a very powerful thing, and it is done for oneself, not for the other person. It is private, and it is done in solitude.

Forgiveness is powerful. It allows us to let go of hurt, and shame. Shame is not a productive emotion. When we feel shame, we make ourselves smaller and less significant. It keeps us from claiming our rightful place in the world, in our relationships, and in our own lives.

We all make mistakes. And we all learn from them. But if we stay emotionally invested in the mistakes, we get stuck and can't move on. Forgiveness is a powerful tool for reconciling my Selves with each other.

When I think about a time in my life when I either did something or didn't do something, and I wish I'd handled it differently, I remember what it felt like. I recall the anger or the pain or the shame or the awkwardness I directed at myself. I really FEEL it, and I understand that the Past Self who experienced that is still a part of me.

Then I remember the information my Past Self had at the time she made that decision. I remember how she felt after she realized it was the wrong call. I allow her to apologize to my Present Self for her mistake. And then I accept her apology and forgive her. I explain to her that I understand why she chose as she did, and that I don't hold it against her any longer. If that mistake wound up teaching me an important lesson, I acknowledge that to my Past Self, and thank her for it.

When I'm working among my Selves, I know that I must issue a forgiveness for every apology. If I am having trouble with the forgiveness, I start by simply loving my Past Self. In my mind and in my heart, I embrace her, enfold her, support her, understand her. She didn't intend to hurt me. Perhaps she was simply mistaken, and she was not even thinking about her Future Self (me), oblivious to the effect she would have. I love her as I would love my best friend. I love her as I want to be loved.

There are very few instances when a sharp "no" is the best way to teach anyone past the toddler stage of development (and even then, there are better ways in many situations). When I tell myself "no", when I engage in negative self-talk and stand in harsh judgment of my own actions, thoughts, and feelings, I am not motivating myself to grow and experience joy.

"No" makes me feel smaller, while "yes" helps me stand taller. When I am holding dialogs with my Past Selves (and remember, even the Me of a moment ago is now a Past Self), I think about reframing judgments into lessons. I focus on why I did something or said something or thought something or felt something, and how I wish I'd behaved differently, and what I can learn for the benefit of my Future Selves. I encourage my Selves, love my Selves, teach my Selves, forgive my Selves, and I find that the Future Selves who come into being are more centered, grounded, and supported.

My shortcut way of remembering all this is: Don't judge. Instead, love. Apply to Selves. Repeat.

CHAPTER 11

Loving My Whole Self, Loving Myself Whole

I have lessons to learn from my Past Selves. I also have the opportunity to heal them from pain and misunderstandings. When I treat my Past Selves with love and understanding and acceptance, I heal past hurts and resentments.

Meditation as a Pathway

I had often thought that I would benefit from a regular meditation practice, but I'd never actually started one. I'd attended meditation workshops now and then over the years, and always enjoyed them, but hadn't made meditation a part of my everyday life.

Then I found an app for my smartphone that has thousands of different types of guided meditations, musical tracks, and the choice of a simple timer, and began sitting in silence for at least five minutes in the morning. It made a big difference in how many times I remembered to notice sensory joys, and how I handled stressful situations. I'm not yet at a point where I meditate every single day, but I do it more often than not.

And I began journaling again. In the past, I had journaled as a way to express strong negative emotions. But now I am recording happiness and spiritual insights as well.

And meditation is my favorite way of facilitating communication among Selves.

When I need to talk to or heal my Selves, I go into a meditative state and "land" on a beach. I sink my feet into the sand, and I raise my face to the sky, which is often at sunrise or sunset. I see and hear and smell the ocean waves. I feel a gentle breeze move through my hair.

Then I turn my attention to the beach, and my Selves begin to appear. I look to the left, and I can see all of my Past Selves. I turn my head and see that all of my potential Future Selves stretch out to my right. We breathe together, we hold space for each other. Sometimes I walk among my Past in order, from my newborn self to my just-a-moment-ago self. I take their hands, I embrace them, I look them in the eyes, and I love them. And they do the same for me.

At different times, a Past or Future Self will assert herself, needing particular attention. I have been on that beach as the Ellen who just became a widow has cried and wailed, and the rest of us surrounded her, lifting her in love and understanding and compassion. I have been on that beach and held my infant self as she wrapped her tiny fist around my finger. I have been on that beach and validated the feelings of a child Ellen who has been teased by siblings or schoolmates, loving her and assuring her that it does get better. I have been on that beach and relived with a teenaged Ellen the first kiss from the boy she liked, the excitement and the feeling that she was beautiful and her future was replete with possibility and acceptance. I have been on that beach when all of us, my Present Self and all of my Past and potential Future Selves, just let go and had a huge dance party together!

Sometimes, my life gets busy or I get distracted, and I forget to meditate for several days in a row. Even though I do have close friends and family, living alone since John died sometimes makes me feel down and lonely. I recently had a week when I was feeling blue, spectacularly unproductive, and very single. I realized it had been a while since I'd meditated, so I sat down for a session, and this is what came to me:

I have been feeling disconnected, drawn in multiple directions, confused, heading towards despair. Conflicting beliefs, conflicting feelings, conflicting cosmological views.

Feeling alone. Feeling adrift. Abandoned.

I need family, friends, a tribe.

I always have my tribe! All of my Selves. I called for them today, told them I needed to be loved. They all showed up, loved me, surrounded me, rocked me. Past and Future Selves buoying and grounding Present Self.

I also felt, strongly, John's love reaching me from across dimensions, across time. All of the love I've ever given or received, and all of the love that I ever will give or receive, is with me here and now.

I just need to remember.

Broken is Perfection

Every now and then, I feel unworthy. I see myself as wanting, or as being a middle-aged widow with everything that was bright and shiny gone forever. I was in that frame of mind when I sat down with my journal and penned this:

Broken is perfection. Just because something is broken, doesn't mean it's not ideal.

It is in that state in this one moment in time, but time is not static, nor is it necessarily linear.

Think of a flower dying, its petals drooping. It is still the embodiment of its perfect "flowerness," or flower essence. It still contains the life cycle, from new seed to production of new seeds. Without fading, bending, it won't fulfill its purpose of creating new flowers and seeding the land.

A Self may not be happy-go-lucky or at ease, but that doesn't make her any less valuable or lovable.

Healing a False Belief: "I Am Not Creative"

I spent most of my life believing that I was not an artistic or creative person. I just accepted that as being true, though I was disappointed and wished it were different. Now, armed with The PPF Method, I set out to examine where that belief had come from. The first insight came from a memory experienced through meditation:

I am in first grade. The smell of chalkdust and mimeograph ink. I sit at my wooden desk, rough from being used by many students before me. The top opens up so I can store my books and lunch inside.

I love going to school. As the youngest child I watched my brother, then my sister, grow up and go off to school. I couldn't wait for my turn. I already know how to read and write.

Today it's raining, so we can't go outside for recess. That's fine with me. I don't much like outside recess – the swings are usually all being used by other kids. We moved to our new house not so long ago, so I don't really have friends here yet.

Mrs. Glennon isn't here today. We have a substitute teacher. She tells us that since we can't go out for recess we'll do an art project instead. That sounds like fun!

She passes out construction paper and paste. We must make a picture with the paper. We can tear it in different shapes but we aren't allowed to cut it.

What shall I make? I look to my left, out the windows at the wet grass, and I think of a dog.

That's what I'll do. I'll make a picture of a French poodle. I can tear up a sheet of paper into small circles. If I can paste them on top of each other just right, they'll be the curly hair that makes up the dog.

I settle in. I pick out a piece of red paper for the background and decide to make a black dog. I tear rough little circles of black, then start to stack them on the red. Hmm. How exactly can I do this to make the shape of the dog? I begin to place the "fur," experimenting.

The substitute is walking up and down, between the desks, looking at what everyone's doing. I'm very intent on figuring out how to manifest my vision of the poodle.

I feel her stop by my desk, watching me. After a few moments, she asks, "What are you making?"

I proudly answer, "A poodle!"

She laughs, loudly. "It looks like a pile of coal!"
I want to pull in on myself, roll into a ball, and fade away.
That was the day I learned I'm not an artist.

I went further, and found other Past Selves who had confirmed this belief.

When I was a young child, my older brother and sister were always making up games for us to play. The one time I remember creating a game, when I was three or four years old, they laughed at me, and they have laughed about how stupid this game was ever since. The rules were simple: everyone runs around in a circle calling out numbers. The first one to yell "nine" wins. What I had in mind but was too young to articulate was that the object of the game was to hold out for as long as possible – to make the game last as long as you could, but still win. Like a game of "chicken" – a game I'd never heard of, so for me it was a unique, original concept. But, because they were older, it wasn't new to them. Simply because I hadn't had as many life experiences, I was necessarily less informed. But I didn't have the perspective to understand this at the time, so I interpreted their reactions as my having a stupid idea. And this was the lesson my Past Self learned: I was fun to play games with, but I wasn't smart enough to be a leader or creative enough to be innovative.

I remember, at five years old or so, sitting outside with my older sister and some of her friends, a rare occurrence for me to be included. We all had coloring books and crayons. I was coloring in the dress of a girl on my page, using a lavender crayon, and for the first time in my life I stayed inside the lines. I also remember using a lighter touch than ever before, and I was coloring very evenly. I was proud of my work, and got some unsolicited compliments from her friends – which caused my sister to get jealous and be mad at me. Lesson learned: Don't improve your artistic abilities if you want to be liked and accepted by your family.

I want to stop, here, and note that in the previous two examples my siblings were young children, themselves. They didn't intentionally set out to hurt me or to teach me these lessons. They're just experiences, which I translated for myself into my way of thinking. I have long since wholeheartedly forgiven both of them for any part they played in my feeling inadequate due to my own personal interpretations of events.

When I was in middle school, I got what I processed as confirmation of my already formed belief about not being artistic or creative. I had a good friend who took private art lessons and could draw very well. I'd never been able to draw well and nobody'd said "we should give Ellen art lessons," so I inferred I wasn't artistic. If I were artistic, I'd be given lessons.

I have had conversations with all of these Past Selves, separately and as a group. We all came to a deep understanding that they came to logical conclusions with the information they had at the time, but that they were all mistaken. They've apologized, I've forgiven, and they have been healed. They no longer feel inadequate, so I no longer automatically assume that I am not creative. And I have taken pottery classes, and stained glass workshops, and drawing lessons, and I've made and sold jewelry, and I write.

I am creative. I am artistic. It is one of my joys.

Adjusting Expectations and Practicing Self-kindness

I was recovering from a stomach virus, finally able to start eating solid food again after three days of being sick. I had awakened feeling more like myself again, more energetic than since before I'd fallen ill. I thought about everything I'd put off but wanted to accomplish this day: clean both bathrooms, flip the mattress, wash and change the bedsheets, and vacuum.

I did a load of laundry, going back and forth between the second floor of the house and the basement. I took a shower. Then I felt completely drained. Even though I had awakened with more energy than I'd had the last few days, I was still weak and tired. That made sense – but I was angry at myself. Not disappointed, not frustrated, but angry, because I felt I should have more control over how I feel.

I finally realized that was ridiculous. I could take steps that would increase my overall energy level – eat the right foods, sleep, exercise – but I couldn't will myself to feel well, or to have stamina right that moment. Once I remembered to take care of myself in a loving way, and forgave my Past Self for getting sick and my Present Self for not being totally well, I was able to recuperate and ease back into everyday life.

Sticking to the Plan

Do I want to stick to the plan? That's a question I ask myself regularly. Remember, the Today Me isn't the same as the Yesterday Me, and sometimes my Present Self sees or hears or learns something new that makes me change my mind about some aspect of my imagined Future.

I am constantly building and adjusting my vision of my future. But I still have a roadmap that will get me where I want to go, even if my destination changes a bit along the way. Without a vision, I would continue to wander here and there, ending up somewhere randomly. It might be wonderful, it might be mediocre, it might be terrible – but the worst part of it would be that it isn't where I wanted to be.

Using The PPF Method to Make Short-term Decisions

A quick dialog between my Present Self and one or more Future Selves can help me make any decision I'm facing. When I am faced with a choice where I can go one of two ways, for example, I close my eyes, take a couple of breaths, and then imagine the Future Self who chose A, and how she feels. Then I imagine the Future Self who chose B, and how that Self feels. This almost always makes it easy for me to make the decision … unless my Present Self strongly wants to choose the one that results in the less joyful Future Self. That's when I need to weigh those options and compromise. Either Present Self or Future Self will not get her way, but as long as I stay aware of this and make the choice consciously and lovingly – and apologize/forgive/thank where appropriate – I am at peace.

One day I was at a restaurant for brunch with a friend, trying to decide whether to order the Macaroni & Cheese or the Eggs Benedict. They both sounded very tasty to my Present Self, and I was having trouble making a choice. So I conjured up my three-hours-from-then possible Future Selves and thought about how they felt. I realized, quickly, that the one who had eaten the Eggs Benedict felt better: she'd felt she had the pleasure of indulging and been nourished with some good protein, but didn't feel nearly as weighed down as the one who'd had the Mac & Cheese, who did enjoy the meal but later felt sluggish as she digested it. So Present Ellen ordered the Eggs Benedict and felt great both in the moment and later on.

As I get more comfortable with the concept of living with and for my many Selves, choices become easier to make. If I'm torn, all I need do is turn to another Self for information.

When I was at a week-long writing retreat in Costa Rica, we had an option of spending one day, on Wednesday, out on an excursion, and I was interested in a cruise down an estuary with a short hike into the forest to see some wildlife. I had planned to go, but had such a fulfilling and productive day of writing on Tuesday that I was loathe to spend the entire next day away from my laptop. I was truly torn, as I had equal desire to go and to stay.

So I meditated, and I decided to talk to two of my possible Thursday Selves: the one who had gone on the excursion, and the one who had stayed to write. The Self who had stayed said she had a great day of writing, and was very pleased with the progress she'd made on her project. She heard her colleagues who had gone on the trip talking about the fun they'd had, but she didn't feel jealous for having missed out.

Then I turned to the Thursday Self who did go on the excursion. She just had a huge smile on her face as she said, "I had a real Costa Rican adventure!"

My choice was clear. Either decision would have been a good one, but the feeling I got from the Self who did the excursion was deep and powerful. So I went, and I did have a real adventure while getting to know some wonderful people better.

As I make decisions, I try always to be aware of why I am choosing as I do, and ask myself, are you serving your Future Self? Providing joy for your Present Self? Is it possible to find a way to do both? Any time that I can build to my Future while enjoying my Present, I feel I am leading the best life.

Dual Future Selves

One day in meditation, I was confronted on my beach by two different Future Ellens.

A visit with two future selves. One is fat, in chronic pain, can barely move. Her life is confined and she has little joy. She suffers. She begs not to Become.

The other is fit, her eyes shine, she smiles. She spends time with friends, she walks, she travels. She wants to Be.

I love them both. I apologize to the first, I promise to act now so that she will not suffer. The second and I are in cahoots, now. Together we will Be.

On the next day, they reappeared.

Right from the beginning, my fit and happy future self was with me, thanking me, meditating with me. The pained and fat future self was there too – the first was nursing the second. I saw that each step I take to a healthier me allows her to fade almost imperceptibly away.

I now do my best to remember both of them every single day, and make the choices that will manifest one and not the other.

Daily Meditations and Affirmations

Meditation has helped me fully incorporate The PPF Method into my life. Being able to go into a quiet, meditative state facilitates the ability to imagine how a particular Future Self will feel, and how to weigh the desires of Present and Future Selves. I know that I am much more consistent about applying the PPF principles when I sit in meditation on a regular basis.

Another good tool is a positive affirmation. I aim to begin every day with this morning affirmation, spoken aloud:

Today I will honor my Present Self while nurturing my Future Self and loving my Past Selves. The future stretches out in front of me and exists all around me in infinite paths. It is up to me, this Present Self, to choose, this day, this moment, which path to travel now, for today.

CHAPTER 12

Revisiting and Revising my Visions of Future Ellen

I had a pretty solid vision of the Future Self I wanted, though some details were still blurry. I knew what kind of house she lived in, what she ate, how her day was structured.

Then I began to take stock, every day, of what I'd done to help manifest her into being. In the evening, as I was getting ready for bed, I'd review my day and ask myself these questions: How did I honor my Past Selves today? How did I experience joy as my Present Self today? How did I forge my Future Selves today?

I would thank myself for even the smallest movement toward my desired future, or the enjoyment of the present, or the healing of the past; and if I'd had a day where I went off track, I would apologize to my Future Self and forgive my Present Self. These thoughts and actions gave me a sense of completion and peace while reminding me of what I truly want to do for myself.

If it was a day when I had made very little progress toward my vision, I tried to think of one thing, however tiny, that might have advanced me on my path. And I didn't think of it as "Well, at least I did that." Instead, I said "Hooray! I took another step." Sometimes I literally pictured confetti swirling around my head as I had a mental party to acknowledge my efforts.

If there were things I intended but didn't get to, I apologized, forgave, and loved myself. When I do that sincerely and with an open heart, from one Self to another, it closes the loop and prevents the "shoulds" from invading. Sometimes I even thank myself for a lesson of feeling bad, as data to use the next time I'm making a choice.

I know that regrets over things undone are useless. I can't change *now* what I haven't done *yet*. I take the lesson and know that my next Self will feel better after the thing is done. And then, when I have the opportunity, I do that thing for her, with all the love I can muster.

Acting As If

Coming up with a vision of my Future Self is all well and good, but when I have trouble thinking of myself in a certain way I need to ignore my doubts and sort of try it on to see how it feels. My vision of my Future Self had me running my own business (which I now do). But I "knew" I wasn't "entrepreneurial" and it was hard to reconcile my desire with my belief.

The first trick was to determine where that voice, the one that said "Oh, don't be silly. You can't run your own business!" came from.

What had my Past Selves experienced that formed this belief? I needed to understand and heal those Selves to quiet the voice.

Then I broke down what it meant to me to be "entrepreneurial" and what I saw as being necessary for running a business. I came to understand that some of what I thought an entrepreneur had to be really had nothing to do with running the type of business I want to have. But even after I'd healed my Past Selves of their false beliefs and redefined "entrepreneurial" for myself, I didn't *feel* like someone who would have her own business.

So, I spent a little more time with my vision of my Future Self and dove deep in to how it felt to be that person: not just what I would do each day, but how I would feel, deep inside, as I did it. And then, once I had that locked in, I spent some time each day acting as if I already felt that way. In only a few weeks the way I saw myself changed, and my vision is manifesting and expanding.

I've often heard the phrase "fake it till you make it." That, to me, is different from Acting As If. Faking it robs me of the chance to be authentic: if I'm faking, I'm not acting like myself. But Acting As If allows me to try on the quality of a Future Self, helping me fully envision that Self, change my mindset, and push through fear.

Positive Self-talk

I am fortunate enough to have people in my life who support my vision, who give me positive feedback and tell me they believe in me. It is a blessing. But it's still important for me to pay attention to how I talk to myself. After all, I am with myself more than anybody else is, and all of the "you've got this, I'm proud of you, you can do it" praise from without is worth almost nothing if all I'm hearing from within is "this is stupid, it's not me, I can't do this."

Anytime I hear negative self-talk in my head, I identify where it's coming from. I heal the Past Self who developed that particular belief. I love her, and forgive her, and embrace her. Then I change the message. Once I do it consciously enough times, it becomes automatic. And I feel unstoppable when I'm singing my own praises!

Thoughts on Failure

I have failed, somewhat spectacularly, a few times in my life. Despite being a very good student most of the time, I have literally failed a class. I have been fired from a job. I have dropped out of a graduate degree program. I felt humiliated and ashamed and worthless each time. But I view failure differently now, and this journal entry reflects that:

If something doesn't work out the first time you try it, you can say you failed to achieve your goal, but it's not true that you are a failure.

Think about this: you're in a hotel room, and you click the remote control because you want to watch television. Nothing happens. Are you a failure because the TV didn't turn on? Do you berate yourself because you didn't make it happen, do you give up immediately?

No. You click the remote again in case you hadn't hit the button hard enough. You try a different button. You aim it differently to try to catch the signal between the TV and the remote. You check to make sure the television is plugged in.

After all that, you may realize that you have failed in your quest to make the TV turn on. But you still wouldn't think of yourself as a failure. You'd seek more information, or turn elsewhere for support (e.g., call the front desk), or you might make the decision that you didn't want to watch that show enough to make it worth your while to get it figured out.

Failing at a particular task does not define you as a failure. If there's a voice in your head telling you that you are a failure, find the Past Self or Past Selves who learned that belief, and heal them.

You don't have a purpose. You have a life. You only must Be. That's it: Be.

You may choose to layer meaning onto your Being.

Thoughts on Fear

Trying new things can be scary, and adopting new ways of thinking definitely stirs up fear in me from time to time. Fear makes me uncomfortable; I've never been a thrill-seeker. I don't like horror movies, I don't understand the attraction to extreme sports. I just don't like to be scared. I meditated on this.

> *It is absolutely normal to feel fear when you are trying something new.*
> *Fear is not the enemy. It is reasonable to be afraid of things like fire, marauding tigers, venomous creatures. Fear protects. Fear maintains. Fear slows you down so that you can assess a situation before jumping into something harmful. Fear creates a force field to keep danger out.*
> *But force fields block you from getting out, as well. Use them judiciously.*
> *When fear appears, stop to ask why. Thank the fear for alerting you to potential danger. Then evaluate, with your reason and your intuition, what the danger is poised to destroy. Is the danger imminent and physically threatening? More often, it is a threat to emotional or intellectual life. Then you must ask yourself whether what will be destroyed is something you would be better off without.*

Fear may be a warning that you are on the edge of your comfort zone. You have the power to acknowledge the fear, thank the fear, then choose an action. Fear will alert you to a threat to the status quo. It's up to you to decide whether the thing that will change is something that is desired by your Future Self.

Fear can be a disguise, used by Judgment. If you're feeling afraid of changing something in your life, examine that feeling closely, and see if it's not true fear but a misguided notion that you're not worthy or that your goals are not correct.

Present Self wants to preserve things as they are. It's what she knows; it's her comfort zone. Future Self wants things to change so that she can emerge according to her dreams. Fear alerts Present Self, but negotiations may result in your being able to dismiss that fear, with gratitude.

If you feel afraid but don't find any true reason to be, breathe deeply. If you add breath to fear, you often transform it into excitement!

Taking my Time

Building a new habit is not the work of a day, or a week. There are some who say it takes 21 days, or instances, to create a new habit. I think it varies, depending on what the habit is, how motivated the individual is to change it, and the nature of what it is you're modifying.

Adding something new to an already established routine, like adding mouthwash to your brushing and flossing habits, is probably going to be pretty easy to do. You might forget once or twice, but you'll figure out a way to remind yourself, like putting the bottle in a particular place, and after a week or two or three it will be as commonplace as the rest of your dental care routine.

But changing something more abstract, like how you talk to yourself or think of yourself or feel about yourself, is going to take more time. It's less like tweaking your dental care routine and more akin to something like learning to drive a car or play a musical instrument.

When you first learn to drive, you are acutely aware of everything you're doing. Where the mirrors are, what everything on the dashboard is telling you, how hard you're pressing on the accelerator and brake pedals, what degree you need to turn the steering wheel, etc. That awareness persists until, one day, you realize you've gotten to the point where you got in the car and drove somewhere, and don't remember actually doing the driving because your mind was elsewhere or you were singing along to the radio. All of the elements that go into driving have become so habitual that you no longer need to constantly think about each one separately. Action has moved from conscious to unconscious through repetition. It has become a gestalt of driving, many parts coming together into a whole.

I know that the same is true of my PPF Method. When I began, I needed to be constantly aware of talking to my Selves, and it felt awkward. But as I continued, I relaxed into it and now it feels like the most natural thing in the world.

Don't Forget Joy!

Oh, right. Joy!

It's so easy to slip back into old habits.

For a few days, I was feeling dark, depressed, and incapable. And I realized I'd forgotten to infuse joy into my life or recognize it when it flitted by.

My joys keep me centered and grounded, and they lift me up so that I can be my best, do my best, and create my best Selves. I've learned that I need to pull out my List of Joys periodically and review it. Are there items I'd forgotten all about again? Do I remember my patterns?

Then I go back to my current vision of my Future Self and make sure I've built joys into her life. If there aren't any, I seriously reconsider why I've decided I want that to be my Future Self at all. Am I envisioning my personal best future, or just a future that I think I should want to have?

There's a phrase, "Tomorrow never comes." Each day is experienced in the now. My Present Self's tomorrow becomes my Tomorrow Self's today, and "tomorrow" actually belongs to the Past Self who was yesterday's Present Self.

Perhaps tomorrow never comes, but my Future Selves will manifest. Taking a mindful, conscious path to bring into being the ones that I purposely envision will lead me to a joyful, centered, and grounded life … unless I wind up only living for my Future Selves, and neglect my Present Self.

If I deny Present Self, if I sacrifice all joy today for the sake of my Future Self, I will most assuredly be living a difficult, dull, unhappy life.

The key, of course, is balance. I want to take advantage of everything I have in the Present to experience joy, whether that is through activity or sensory experience or spirituality. At the same time, I can take steps to create my Future Self as I envision her. Doing so makes even the sacrifices joyful. For example, if I want my Future Self to take a vacation then I may need to save some money for that. Creating a budget and sticking to it, even when it means passing up some momentary pleasure, can create great joy when I know I am paying it forward to myself.

And when my Future Self acknowledges my Present Self for doing so, and expresses gratitude and love, that in itself brings joy to both.

I don't spend every minute of every day serving only my Future Selves. Enjoying the moment and making great memories is also something that my Future Selves will be able to take part in, because my Present Self is my Future Self's Past Self – and all of my Past Selves are always part of who I am.

CHAPTER 13

I am a Work in Progress

I'd love to be able to say that I had my realization about Past, Present, and Future Selves, developed The PPF Method, and have been applying it consistently in my life ever since.

But that's not how it's going.

It's been a process to get used to this, and I've spent weeks thinking about my Selves, using the construct to arrange my life in a way that brings me joy and keeps me on the path to achieving all of my dreams. And then I've spent weeks falling back into old habits, having Present Self take over exclusively, and stalling on the way to my goals. When that happens, I begin again by resuming my daily review of my day at bedtime, with its gratitude, apologies, and forgiveness.

Such is life, such is being a human with flaws. The key – and I'm very proud of this – is that I haven't jettisoned the idea because of temporary "failure" in applying it. It's a method that works well for me, and it's a method that works well for the clients I've taught it to. So I persist. And as time goes on, I become more and more consistent and aware, and the more I negotiate among my Selves the more natural and automatic it becomes.

I am kinesthetic by nature: my memory has always focused more on feelings than on other senses. And as I work with The PPF Method, I've found that my visions and intentions are moving more toward feelings rather than details. When I think about my ideal Future Self, I focus more now on how she feels and how she perceives herself, and a bit less on what she does. That resonates with me, it feels natural, and it's an easy way for me to lock on to my desires.

My visions are becoming more about Being than Doing.

Beautiful. Peaceful. The sensation of floating in a sensory deprivation tank, freed from all physical constraints.

Needed to be loved, sent out the call, and it was answered a thousandfold. All of my selves, past and future, surrounding me, holding me, supporting me, lifting me. Simultaneously grounded and lifted.

So much love. I attune myself to love. I attune to the light. We can attach, attune, to all energies – make the choice. We are the Universe, it is us, all of it. Choose the vibration.

Love. Love softens the edges while strengthening the core. The softness serves others, the strength – the bright fire of the core – grounds and provides the source for all giving.

Focus less on the mechanics of creating future selves, and more on the intention, the vibration, the love. Attune to the love. Attune to the light. The rest will fall into place.

Focus on the person you want to Be, rather than the things you think she needs to do. Be loving, Be compassionate, Be kind, Be vibrant, Be a connector, Be creative, Be knowledgeable, Be fun. Be known.

Be.

Don't get distracted by expectations of entrepreneurship, or by achievements. It's not about achieving, it's about becoming.

The more I live with The PPF Method, the more I trust myself.

I feel lifted, and filled with light. Ready to spread kindness and compassion and healing.

But then I feel doubt – no, mistrust – in myself: my Future Selves not trusting that this Present Self will serve them.

But that is unfair. Past Selves may have let them down, but this Present Self, every Present Self, is pure. Innocent. Not to be judged for actions of the Past. The fastest way to make someone untrustworthy is to mistrust them without cause.

Now I see my two Future Selves, the healthy and unhealthy. They understand and are smiling patiently, waiting, loving me. Trusting in me. I will not let them down. All is perfect.

The PPF Method is powerful, but it is not magic. I still have issues to work out within myself – issues around resistance and confidence and belief. But if I love myself enough, I can love myself into joy.

What is blocking me, my Present Self, from taking actions that will manifest my centered, soulful, successful, happy future self?

Why do I resist? And just sit?

The Future Self I imagine is sanguine, lithe, peaceful, confident. But now I realize there are barriers to be broken through, lessons to be learned, discomfort to be tolerated in order to get from here to there. Can I love her enough to do the work?
Love is not a feeling.
Love is an action.
Love by doing.

I am still a work in progress, far from embodying the full vision of my ideal future self. But that vision is constantly evolving, and I am learning and anchoring in more deeply. I find that it's hard not to fall back to my old habit of floating through life.

What helps most is daily meditation and journaling. When I skip two or three days in a row, I easily lose sight of my destination and tend to start bobbing about aimlessly again. I start living more by avoidance than intention, because life can feel hard. On my own, creating something new, building a new career aren't things that come naturally.

But I'm not fighting it. Resistance only fuels those "shoulds" and recriminations. Instead, I become aware again, refocus my vision of my Future Self, set aside meditation and writing time, and take stock at the end of each day. The mosaic pieces are beginning to form a beautiful image.

I apologize, and forgive, and heal, and celebrate. And I move closer to the Self I most want to manifest, the one who is serene yet energetic, who inspires hope in others, who is healthy and fit, and who lives consciously with joy.

Manifesting My Best Future, Choice by Choice

When I take stock at the end of each day, when I take time to meditate each morning, when I express gratitude, and forgive, and apologize, when I implement The PPF Method to make every choice, I move closer and closer to becoming the Future Ellen that always carries joy in her heart, brings compassion and kindness to others, and feels fulfilled by the life's purpose she has chosen for herself.

And when I use The PPF Method consistently, and I intentionally think about my Past, Present, and Future Selves, this is what appears in my meditation journal:

I am an expression of the Universe. I am a perfect expression of the Universe. Let me be an instrument of light, of love.

Allow. Allow the light of the Source to shine in me and through me and from me. Allow me to inspire others to shine, to be at peace, to recognize themselves as perfect expressions of the Universe.

Who is Present Ellen? How does she intend to Be?

Present Ellen is light of spirit. Present Ellen is preparation Ellen – preparing herself and her environment for the week ahead, and beyond.

I am never alone. I am loved and lifted and informed by all my infinite selves.

I am light. There is light that shines within me and through me and radiates from me, and that light is One with the light of the Source and Destination. I am connected.

I am light
I am love
I am everything

I am the heart of the Universe
The Universe is in the heart of me

Remember. Remember!
Open, and Allow.

I choose Life. I choose Love. I choose Health. I choose Joy!

EPILOGUE

Gratitude and Trade-offs

I am grateful, beyond words, for the time I had with John. For the great love and acceptance and humor and passion that filled our relationship. That I am still a vessel for that love, and that the despair I sank into when he died has been transformed into even more love, and service to others. I am grateful for the beautiful energy of the universe, for the myriad ways it is seen and expressed and manifested. I am grateful for my pen and paper and keyboard, and for words that can conjure feelings and images. I am grateful for light and love and air and for having lived one more day. I am grateful for love from family, good friends, my author community, and my cat. I am grateful for the comforts of home. I am grateful for breath and tears and touch and music and connection. I am grateful for my struggles and the lessons I have learned and have yet to learn.

John is, still, a vital part of my everyday life. I think of him all the time; I have conversations with him in my head; I see his expressions of wonder and doubt and support and caution and love and laughter.

I love my new normal. I feel more grounded and centered, and my days are filled with joys tiny and expansive. I am realizing dreams that I'd forgotten I'd ever had.

But the truth is, I would trade it all in a heartbeat for even one more day with John here, by my side. I miss his voice. I miss his touch.

And I am grateful.

ABOUT THE AUTHOR

Ellen Landsburg Monsees is a heart-centered but practical author, speaker, and coach. She delights in her role as guide and companion to her clients on their journey to a more grounded, healthy, and desired version of themselves. Her own experience has taught her that grief need not be forever and recovery is possible. She believes that joy outweighs sorrow in the long run and  in the moment - if you learn to harness it and revel in it. She knows that life can be happy and hopeful again even after tragedy.

A woman of eclectic interests, Ellen has worked at a major charitable foundation and several institutions of higher learning in positions spanning information technology, library management, communications, and donor relations. She holds a BA in Psycholinguistics from Swarthmore College, an MS in Information Studies from Drexel University, and Certification as an Advanced Grief Recovery Method Specialist® from the Grief Recovery Institute®. She enjoys reading, board games, singing, making jewelry and pottery, and relaxing at home with her cat. She resides in the suburbs of Philadelphia.

CONNECT WITH ME!

MoveBeyondLoss@gmail.com
www.ellenmonsees.com
484-441-3954

Coaching programs available in my office in Media, Pennsylvania; online; or at your event:

The Grief Recovery Method®:
- teaches you tools for completing your relationship to the emotional pain, isolation, and loneliness caused by grief and loss,
- provides strategies for putting unfulfilled hopes, dreams, and expectations to rest,
- returns your ability to think of happy memories without being overcome by pain and sadness.

This may be the right program for you if:
- you have experienced any of the more than forty life experiences that may result in feelings of loss and grief,
- you are feeling emotionally stuck in a rut,
- you aren't connecting with others on as deep or intimate a level as you wish,
- you avoid new relationships out of fear of experiencing the pain of loss,
- you find yourself focusing exclusively on how your loved one died, rather than how they lived,
- you are waiting for time to heal your sorrow,
- you have a troubled relationship with a living person, such as a parent, who hasn't fulfilled your hopes, dreams, or expectations for your interactions.

PLEASE NOTE: If you aren't able to focus sufficiently to do the reading and homework for The Grief Recovery Method, you may want to start with Stepping out of Grief (below).

Ways this program may be experienced:
- in person, one-on-one,
- in person, as part of a group,
- in person, as part of a group specifically focused on pet loss,
- online, one-on-one (computer with high-speed internet connection required).

Helping Children Deal with Loss (a program affiliated with The Grief Recovery Method):
- teaches you how to help children when they are grieving, so that they have the tools for dealing with loss in a healthy way for the rest of their lives.

This may be the right program for you if:
- you are the parent or guardian of a child/children who have experienced any of the more than forty life experiences that may result in feelings of loss and grief,
- you are a teacher, school administrator, pediatric health worker, or are in another position that interacts with children who may experience grief.

Ways this program may be experienced:
- in person, one-on-one,
- in person, as part of a group.

Stepping out of Grief:
- provides a safe environment for taking the first baby steps out of pain and grief,
- teaches strategies for dealing with feelings and situations common to many new grievers,
- addresses issues relating to anxiety, dealing with physical belongings, self-care, and keeping your loved one's memory alive.

This may be the right program for you if:
- you have lost someone who was part of your daily living, especially a member of your household,
- you are having trouble with everyday tasks,
- your loss has made you feel disconnected from your life,
- you are experiencing a roller coaster of emotions and don't have the ability to concentrate.

PLEASE NOTE: This program is intended to be a precursor, but not a prerequisite, to The Grief Recovery Method.

Ways this program may be experienced:
- in person, one-on-one,
- in person, in a small (2-3 people) group,
- in person, in a larger group at your event,
- online, one-on-one (computer with a high-speed internet connection required).

Stepping into Joy: The PPF Method™ for Manifesting Your Most Joyful Self:
- introduces The PPF Method,
- provides strategies for making choices that serve your best self,
- allows you to create a new normal that is driven by intentional joy.

This may be the right program for you if:
- you have recovered from grief and find your old life no longer fits,
- you are experiencing a shift in perspective or lifestyle and want to live with purpose,
- you have lost your "old normal" involuntarily, or you have abandoned it deliberately, but you don't know what to do next,
- you find you are simply going through the motions of life, and want to find meaning, joy, and purpose,
- you have ever looked around you and thought, "I just don't feel like myself. How did this become my life?"

Ways this program may be experienced:
- in person, one-on-one,
- in person, in a small (2-3 people) group,
- online, one-on-one (computer with a high-speed internet connection required).

Other online workshops are currently being developed; check my website or sign up for my mailing list for notification of new offerings!

www.ingramcontent.com/pod-product-compliance
Lightning Source LLC
Chambersburg PA
CBHW050201130526
44591CB00034B/1688